DADDY'S SCRAPBOOK

Henry Kimbro

Of The Negro Baseball League

A Daugther's Perspective

HARRIET KIMBRO-HAMILTON

IN DUE SEASON PUBLISHING

For information contact :
Dr. Harriet Kimbro-Hamilton at
henrykimbro12@gmail.com

Book Layout and Cover Design by
Enger Lanier Taylor for In Due Season Publishing

ISBN: 978-0-9727456-4-2
Library of Congress Control Number: 2015949746
In Due Season Publishing, Huntsville, Alabama

CONTENTS

FOREWORD

Negro Leaguer Jim Zapp

When I was stationed at Staten Island Navy Base in New York, New York, I played with the Baltimore Elite Giants baseball team on the weekends. The first person I met on the team was Henry Kimbro. He didn't say much and I didn't expect him to. We were both from Nashville, Tennessee and had that in common. A lot of guys on the team didn't like Kimbro because he was a loner. You never saw Kimbro after a game, only before and during the game, even on the road. Later in life, after we were retired Kimbro, Butch McCord, Sidney Bunch, and I would hang out together at The Old Negro League Sports Shop on Jefferson

Street in Nashville, Tennessee. The owner, Larry Walker, loved hearing our baseball stories and how we teased each other about our moments in the league. On many occasions we had people come to the shop just to meet us and get our autographs. We had good times there.

I loved playing baseball. It gave me the chance to travel all over the states and out of the states to the Dominican Republic. I played with guys that went on to Major League Baseball like Willie Mays, Joe Black, Roy Campanella, and Artie Wilson. Satchel Paige was as good as they say. Once I asked Hank Thompson of the Kansas City Monarch, if Major League Pitchers were throwing as hard as Satchel. He said, they were throwing as hard, but their ball didn't look as small as Satchel's ball.

During my career, I played with several teams. My favorite team was the Birmingham Black Barons in 1948. The owner, Tom Hayes, did everything first class. The manager, Lorenzo Piper Davis, was the best. He got the best out of his players. The Birmingham Community both black and white gave the Barons a lot of support at Rickwood Field. We played our games in front of thousands of fans.

When Jackie Robinson signed with the Brooklyn Dodgers, I was one of those who believed that baseball would never be integrated. Now I know Negro League Baseball helped make that change come. To me, if integration of baseball had come earlier, a lot of white ball players would never have played. Players like Cool Papa Bell, Josh Gibson, and many more including Henry Kimbro would be in their place.

I still remember the names of the guys I played with. Most of those guys are gone now. I miss those guys. It was a special time playing in the Negro League. Looking back, I wouldn't trade it for anything.

Jim Zapp

Baltimore Elites (45-36, 50-51, 54)

(Courtesy of Jim Zapp)

Introduction

When my father, Henry Kimbro, died in 1999, my mother gave me an old tattered scrapbook and told me to do something with it. It was a sixty-year-old collection of pictures, original articles, and miscellaneous items my father had collected. These items were related to his playing experiences in Negro League Baseball. The items in the scrapbook were quite impressive; especially considering this was Daddy's collection, not my mom's. I'd never known him to collect anything; so apparently, the items contained within the covers were important to him. The scrapbook inspired me to share his story.

When my mother gave me all of his books on the Negro League, I was again inspired. These were all books I'd given him, with the exception of one, the first book he received. That one came from an avid Negro League fan who grew up in the Washington, DC area watching Negro League Baseball games. Judge A.A. Birch had made history himself, becoming the first African-American Chief Justice to serve on the Tennessee Supreme Court. The book he'd sent my father was called *The Negro Baseball Leagues: A Photographic History*, by Phil Dixon and Patrick J. Hannigan.

Actually, I'd known about this book for some time. One day when I was at Hadley Park (in Nashville) playing tennis, Judge Birch, also a tennis player, approached me and said, "I have a book for your father." On the first page of the book Judge Birch wrote, "To Mr. Kimbro, a true pioneer, this book belongs on your shelf, not on mine, best wishes."

Daddy was pleasantly surprised when I gave him the book, reading it over and over again. Seeing his response, I began giving him books about the Negro League as presents on his birthdays, or for Christmas. He loved to read, and to watch western movies, but he got a real kick out of reading about the Negro League.

The second book he received was *The Biographical Encyclopedia of the Negro Baseball Leagues*, by James A. Riley. Before giving him this book, I read it. I was surprised to read the part that described him as an "evil man." My mother did once describe him as steel on the outside but a good-hearted man on the inside. And, I admit he had an extra-short fuse in dealing with things he didn't like. My siblings, Larry and Phillip, and I grew up knowing that. Even so, my father wasn't an evil man, or even a mean-spirited man. Yet the writer of this book had called him evil.

When I presented him with the second book as a gift, I brought to his attention the part that described him as an evil man. Expecting him to get mad and blow a fuse, I was shocked when he just chuckled and said, "Oh, I don't pay no attention to that stuff." From that point I was determined to look into this further, because clearly I'd missed something. Just as clearly, my father wasn't going to talk about it anymore.

As I continued to buy Negro League books for him — and read through them before giving them to him — I began having conversations with him about what was written. This wasn't an easy task; Daddy was a man who spoke if he had something to say, and if he didn't have anything to say he wouldn't. He began to open up, slowly, about his baseball career.

While I was growing up in his house, he never mentioned or shared any of his history as a professional baseball player. I thought the man had never been outside of Nashville. My mother explained it as the reticence of a man focusing on making a living for his family. He did that quite well, as a businessman who owned and ran his own taxicab company. His workday started at dawn and ended late in the evening seven days a week. In fact, I was close to graduating from high school before I knew anything about Daddy's past. It was like learning the secret identity of someone you thought you knew, and finding out they had another life.

One day when I was at his cab station, I met a man named Butch McCord. Daddy didn't go into any details of who he was and how he knew him, but I could tell they were good friends. At one point, Mr. McCord turned to me and said, "Did you know that your daddy was a heck of a baseball player?"

I assumed he was referring to the local baseball teams my father played with when my brother and I would watch him at Hadley Park. I was wrong. Mr. McCord went on to say that my daddy played with the Baltimore Elite Giants, a professional team in the Negro Baseball league, and made the All-Star team a couple of times. Mr. McCord knew this because he and Daddy had played with the team. He finished by saying, "Ask your daddy about it." I did. My father responded with, "Yeah, I played a little bit." Daddy definitely underplayed his answer. And I'll always be grateful to Mr. McCord for letting me know that.

During my research, I found my father's talent was well respected, and he was considered one of the best players in the League, yet people often referred to him as the "bad boy" of Negro League Baseball. The most hurtful statement I read about my father was written in an article published following his death: where he was called the Black Ty Cobb of Negro League Baseball. From what I've read about Ty Cobb, this was not a compliment about his talent but a reference to him as a person. Daddy was, in his own words, a man "with a peppery temperament" at times, who was also a man of few words by choice. [1]

Of course, I saw my father very differently than others did. To me my father was an exceptional man, who, with only a 6th-grade education, educated and trained himself in skills he needed to succeed. He was a good provider for his family, and sent four of his five children to college. Despite numerous racial and educational barriers, he became a successful businessman for 22 years.

The intention of this book is to reflect on my father's career through his scrapbook; profile his life through family memories from my older brother Larry, my younger brother Phillip, my younger sister Maria, my mother, and myself; and share stories from those who played with him, and against him. My hope is that this book will be regarded as an accurate portrait of my father, and that history will respect his contributions, and the legacy he left.

Judge A.A. Birch and I
(Courtesy of Author)

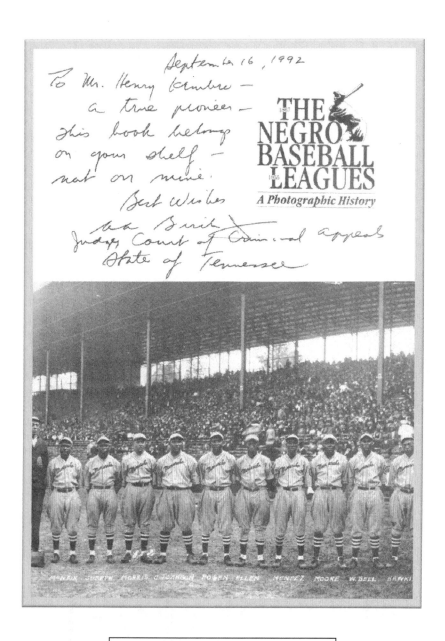

Judge A.A. Birch Note
(Courtesy of Amereon House Publishers)

CHAPTER 1

From Boyhood to Manhood

Henry Allen Kimbro lived a long and eventful life full of mostly fulfilled dreams. Born February 10, 1912, the fourth of nine children of Sallie King Kimbro and Willie Kimbro, Henry was raised where he was born, in Nashville, Tennessee, the county seat of Davidson County. The Kimbros came from the Chapel Hill area, where my grandmother Sallie is buried, south of Nashville. Young Henry's father supported the family as a farmer, growing crops for Walden College, and he worked at Mount Olive Cemetery as a groundskeeper. When my father was 17 years old, Grandpa Willie died of gum disease. Grandma Sallie, at age 47, had to raise her children on her own.

With both of my parents being dead, I wanted to know more about my father's childhood and my grandparents. So, in the summer of 2007, I went to visit my Aunt Louise, who was 89 years old at the time and the only one of my father's siblings still alive. What I found was that she was more like her brother Henry in personality than she cared to admit. She shared pictures and told me stories about them growing up, saying that life was hard for everyone, especially after their father died. She often wondered how Grandma Sallie made it during those times, supporting nine children on her own. "She (Grandma Sallie) did laundry for the white folks with everybody working some kind of job. They never went hungry." [1]

Aunt Louise described Grandma Sallie as a strong-minded, no-nonsense woman who raised her children to mind, be respectful, and work hard. She also added that there was no such thing as any of her children not doing what they were told. Grandma Sallie was a deeply religious woman, who often hosted the church women's bible study in her home. She served on the Mother Board of Mount Gilead Church in south Nashville. She also meant business in all she did, and her nearly six-foot height and strong facial features helped support her serious attitude. My mother spoke of how physically strong Grandma Sallie was, and I was aware my grandmother was a major influence in my father's life. Ms. Scales, who lived across the street from Grandma Sallie's house and was one of her oldest friends, described my father as "a good son to his mother."[2]

I was three years old when my Grandma Sallie died, and only vaguely remember her. I do remember that after her death, there were issues between my father and his siblings over Grandma Sallie's house. According to Daddy, Grandma Sallie wrote a piece of paper that gave the house to him. Her document was not a legal will, however, and Daddy's siblings wanted him to buy them out of what they felt was their part of the house. Even so, he felt they should have honored their mother's wishes.

The house eventually went to auction. Daddy got his lawyer to bid on the house for him, and got it. After that, we never saw or spoke to anyone in his family again until we were older. They just disappeared from our lives. I asked Daddy about it once, and he did not want to speak of it. I know his refusal to speak was deliberate on his part. Later, my mother confirmed he wanted nothing to do with his family for putting him and us through the drama. We never again went over to our Aunt Louise's house for Sunday dinners with the family. We never saw our cousins again at family functions. No one from the family ever just stopped by the house again. In fact, when I was leaving my Aunt Louise's house from my visit that summer, her last words to me were, "Alexina (she always called me by my middle name because she said it was a pretty name), come see me again, I don't want to lose you again."[3]

Growing up in the south, there were childhood experiences that shaped my father's life, and some of them were not happy ones. One was related to education. When Negro League history was rediscovered, those players still alive were sought-after for interviews, especially those like Daddy, who were considered the stars of the league. When asked why other players perceived him as mean, evil, and a loner, he said it was because of his lack of education, which ended at the 6th grade. In most interviews given, he talked about his lack of education as one of the worst things that ever happened to him. During his elementary years, he attended a school near his community, but because his family lived outside the Nashville city limits, he could not attend the closest city school. To continue his education in the 7th-grade, he would have to attend a Davidson County school, and the nearest black county school was 12 miles one way. Transportation wasn't available to him, so he would have to walk to school and back. Of this, Daddy said, "You know we walked everywhere in those days, but 24 miles a day was too hard."[4] So he had to let go of the dream of continuing to the seventh grade and beyond.

Not having the opportunity to get an education "tore me to pieces," he said, and constantly explained to all his children why an education was important. According to him, education was the key to a better life, and without it, you were limited for the rest of your life. To him, you see, an educated person knew how to use words, how to write words, and how to speak words to express himself to other people. In his view, an educated person was not easily fooled or taken advantage of. Daddy felt vulnerable about this, especially growing up in the south, where he often saw black folks taken advantage of by white folks because, as he put it, "the black folks just didn't know any better."[5] This greatly angered and frustrated him. This is actually what led to his conservative demeanor in communicating with people. When he had something to say he would say it; if he did not have anything to say he would not say anything.

Daddy had a temper. It was easy for him to get angry. It was easy for him to go on the offensive with people and it was easy for him to dismiss people and just not be bothered with them. I believe that had a lot to do with how he dealt with experiences growing up that frustrated and angered him. This, combined with his temper, might well have led to the way those who wrote about him perceived him.

When Daddy ended his education, he got a job at a filling (gas) station, where he cleaned up and did other chores for seven dollars a week. An Irishman called Mr. Byrd owned the station. Mr. Byrd had two sons who also worked at the station. Both boys were older than my father. He told me that both boys would fight him and call him a nigger. Mr. Byrd knew this was going on, but did little about it except verbally warn his boys to stop picking on my dad. Daddy said he needed that job, so he was not going to quit. He decided he needed to get physically stronger, so he could whip both boys when they messed with him. First, he got a ladder and set it across a stack of several tires, and then he would swing across the ladder to build up his arm strength. To build up his legs, he used old ropes to jump rope. On top of that, he did exercises like pushups and jumping jacks and the like. I asked him if that worked, and he smiled and said, "Oh yeah, that worked." Apparently, it worked well. He whipped both of those brothers, and they left him alone after that. He was not fired for beating up the owner's sons. Mr. Byrd was a fair man, as fair as a white man could be to a black boy during those times.[6] I suspect he had a silent ear when my dad got his sons back. In fact, Daddy kept working for Mr. Byrd well into his twenties. During those years he learned about cars, how to repair them and keep them running. These skills no doubt contributed to his later business success.

Although he spent most of his life working on cars, driving taxicabs, and owning a taxicab business, he also had other interesting jobs. My older brother Larry spoke of Daddy running (driving) bootleg moonshine to some parts of West Tennessee, and he had a reputation as a skilled driver. He also worked as a bouncer at the New Era Club. The club owner, William "Sou" Bridgeforth, a popular black businessman in Nashville, was the last owner of the Baltimore Elite Giants, and was known for hiring baseball players for his nightclub.[7]

While playing sandlot baseball in the Nashville city parks, Daddy was noticed by Tom Wilson, who was one of the wealthiest black businessmen in Nashville, and considered the architect of the development of black professional baseball in Nashville and the South. At the time, Wilson owned the Nashville Elite Giants, a Negro League baseball team. He invited my dad to play on his team, but Daddy turned him down the first time. Daddy said, "I ain't never been nowhere like that so I can't see me leaving Nashville to go play like that."[8] In fact, it was Jim Taylor of the Chicago American Giants who recruited Daddy to play with the team Taylor organized to barnstorm throughout the South for a short period. When Daddy returned to Nashville, he accepted Tom Wilson's offer to play with his team. Thus began his long baseball career with Tom Wilson's Elite Giants team as they moved from Nashville, to a couple of other cities, and finally to Baltimore, Maryland.

Earlier in Daddy's baseball career, he met and fell in love with his first wife, Nellie Bridges. They married and their first child, my stepbrother, Larry Kimbro, was born March 10, 1936. During the early years of the marriage, Daddy was constantly away from home playing baseball. Larry remembered that our father and his mother fought all the time. Many issues, in fact, put Daddy and Nellie at odds with each other, and they eventually divorced. After the divorce, Grandma Sallie had my father and Larry living in her house, but Daddy traveled a lot due to his baseball career, so Larry was raised mostly by Grandma Sallie. Years after the divorce, Nellie had a mental breakdown that put her in a mental institution periodically throughout her life, and that was where she died. As much as he loved playing baseball, Daddy did regret the times he had to leave Larry. Although Nashville continued to be his home, Tom Wilson's Elite Giants were moved to several cities before moving to their permanent home of Baltimore. Larry told me once that the only time he saw Daddy shed a tear was when he had to leave him to go play baseball.[9]

During Daddy's early years in Baltimore with the team, he had a romantic relationship with a woman there. From that relationship came his second child, who was born out of wedlock, my stepsister Geraldine. My father never was a part of her life as she was growing up in Baltimore. I remember meeting my stepsister once when she came to spend the summer of 1962 with our family. I was about nine years old; Geraldine was a teenager, about 16 years old. She stayed in my room and we had some good times, except when she was hanging out with other teenagers in the neighborhood. Then, she did not want to be bothered with me. While staying with us she never warmed up to our dad, though Daddy was especially nice to, patient with, and tolerant of her. At the time, I could see hurt on both their faces.

When Geraldine left, Daddy reached into his pocket and gave her what I think was a hundred dollars, then hugged her and said goodbye. She hugged him back. At the time, I just wanted to know why he did not give Phillip and me money like that. My mother later explained that he loved Geraldine as much as he loved all his children, and it hurt him that he would never be part of her life as a real father. After that, I did not pursue the money issue anymore, because I appreciated having a father that was part of my life. During that summer visit with Aunt Louise, she gave me the only picture she had of Geraldine, one from when she was three years old. I would love to see my big sister again, but unfortunately, no one in the family can tell me her last name; by the time I became interested in finding her, both of my parents had passed. It was something I know Daddy regretted, not seeing his daughter Geraldine ever again.

Through his journey into manhood, Daddy was blessed to have a mother who instilled in him the lessons of hard work, responsibility, and self-discipline while growing up in the South of the 1920s. She molded a boy who overcame the cruelties of discrimination and the heartbreak of broken dreams to become a strong-willed man who refused to let life defeat him. A woman with strong religious faith, Grandma

Sallie was his best example of how to rise above your circumstances.

Just as Grandma Sallie gave him the foundation into manhood, it was Tom Wilson, the owner of the Nashville Elite Giants, who provided my father and many others with a life-changing opportunity to become part of the Negro League, and history. In a previous publication, I wrote about Tom Wilson and his impact.

Born in Atlanta, Georgia in 1890, he moved to Nashville with his parents where they both attended Meharry Medical College and became medical doctors (Lanctot 79). An average baseball player in his youth, Wilson nevertheless loved the game, later becoming associated with Nashville's Capital City League (CCL), a semi-professional team in Nashville.

Wilson's vision of promoting black baseball in Nashville was sparked in 1914 when Rube Foster and the Chicago American Giants came to Nashville to play exhibition games against the Nashville Capital City League ("Southern Stars" 1). In 1918, Wilson acquired a semi-professional team called the Nashville Standard Giants, which later would be called the Nashville Elite Giants (Riley 875).

Wilson soon began to mold Nashville into a mecca for black baseball by recruiting the best local talent. Robert Abernathy, a former Negro League player, said, "Wilson found plenty of talent for his team...recruiting Nashville kids who had grown up with the game" (qtd. In Horick 24). Throughout the years, Wilson had many of the most talented local ballplayers in baseball play on his team, providing the homegrown talent in Nashville and its surrounding area with a chance to play professional baseball. In bringing professional baseball to Nashville's African-American community, Wilson jumped-started the careers of a number of significant local players in the various Negro Leagues who would later gain national fame.

Another native Nashvillian to benefit from Wilson's vision was National Baseball Hall of Famer Norman Thomas "Turkey" Stearns. Stearns played baseball at Nashville's Pearl High School, and later joined the Nashville Elite Giants in 1920. After a year with Wilson's Elite Giants, Stearns embarked on a twenty-two year career, playing with Negro League teams as an outfielder and first baseman (Riley 739). Another native Nashvillian, James "Junior" Gilliam, started his baseball career playing for the Nashville Black Vols (1945), moving the following years, at seventeen, to Wilson's Baltimore Elite Giants. In 1951, he was recruited and signed by the Dodger organization and sent to their minor-league team in Montreal. In 1953, he was moved up to play for the Brooklyn Dodgers, and during his initial season, he earned the National League's Rookie of the Year Award. His major-league career spanned from 1953-1966 (Riley 319).

Other significant local talent signed by Wilson included pitcher Robert "Schoolboy" Griffith, who played for Wilson's teams in Nashville, Columbus,

Washington Elite Giants, and Baltimore (Riley 340). Exposed to baseball as a youth in Nashville, Robert Abernathy of Columbia, Tennessee played for three teams and was known as a line-drive hitter who could play defense well (Riley 26). An outstanding all around athlete, Wesley "Doc" Dennis, also of Nashville, would eventually become as well known as one of the city's most outstanding golfers. He began his career with the Baltimore Elite Giants, later moving on to play with the Philadelphia Stars and the Birmingham Black Barons (Riley 229). Seven time Negro League All-Stars Burris "Wild Bill" Wright of Milan, Tennessee, played for Wilson for most of his career. Wright later left the Negro League to play in the Mexican League, later earning induction into the Mexican Baseball Hall of Fame (Riley 881). Finally, Clinton "Butch" McCord of Nashville, continues to be well respected as a leading advocate for Negro League Baseball history. He began his career with the Nashville Black Vols in 1947, joining the Baltimore Elite Giants the following year. After leaving the Negro Leagues in 1950, McCord enjoyed a long minor league career, winning two minor league batting titles and two Silver Gloves for fielding excellence.

In the 1920s, Wilson's Nashville Elite Giants competed regionally in the Southern Baseball League against such teams as the Atlanta Black Crackers and the Birmingham Black Barons. Elite Giant games provided a popular destination for Nashville's African-American community, prompting the owner to build Wilson Park, the first black-owned ballpark, in the south, in 1928. Providing a significant economic boost to Nashville's African American community, "the new facility was located in the Trimble Bottom section of Nashville near the Old Meharry Medical College and Walden College. It was north of the fairgrounds and near Second and Fourth Avenue in South Nashville. It was built to accommodate 8000 fans. Wilson Park was located in Nashville's largest Negro community" ("Southern Stars" 2). McCord would later lead a successful campaign to erect a historical marker on the site of Wilson Park, bring overdue recognition to this significant figure in Tennessee and Negro League Baseball history.

Although the Nashville Elite Giants remained financially successful in the league during the 1930s, other league teams were financially strained with the travel distance to Nashville. Cum Posey, owner of the Homestead Grays advised Wilson to move "to a Northern city or else join the South League (qtd. in Lanctot, 35). Wilson began plans to move his team to the north. He initially planned to move the Nashville Elite Giants to Detroit, Michigan and lease Hamtramck Stadium, but the lease plans fell through in 1935, and the Elites moved instead to Columbus, Ohio and became the Columbus Elite Giants (Lanctot 46).

Constantly looking for lucrative markets, Wilson moved his Elite giants from Columbus to Washington, DC in 1936, where they won the first half of the Negro National Championships with a 14-10 record (Riley 820). In 1937, Richard Powell, a baseball promoter in Baltimore, Maryland, convinced Wilson to move to Baltimore, where the Baltimore Elite Giants would overtake the Homestead Grays for the top spot in the National Negro League in 1939. After the National Negro League folded, the team joined Negro American League and won the league championship in 1949 (Riley 50).

On the national level, Wilson played a major role in the growth of the National Negro League. As the elected President of the league from 1938-1947, Wilson initiated the successful East-West All-Star game, increased baseball players salaries, and contributed to the overall prosperity of the league during his tenure (Southern Stars 3). When Jackie Robinson broke the color barrier in 1947, many were prepared to realize the opportunity due to the efforts of men like Tom Wilson who, with others, helped to build the bridge that made the dream possible.[10]

Aunt Louise and I
(Courtesy of Author)

Aunt Louise, Phillip and I
(Courtesy of Author)

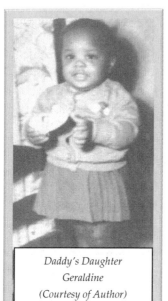

Daddy's Daughter
Geraldine
(Courtesy of Author)

Larry Kimbro & Nellie (Mother)
(Courtesy of Author)

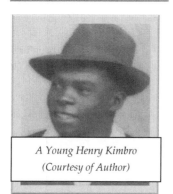

A Young Henry Kimbro
(Courtesy of Author)

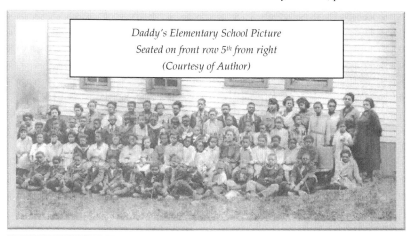

Daddy's Elementary School Picture
Seated on front row 5th from right
(Courtesy of Author)

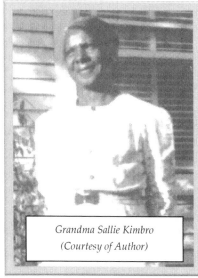

Grandma Sallie Kimbro
(Courtesy of Author)

Henry and Erbia Kimbro
(Courtesy of Author)

My Brother Larry and I
(Courtesy of Author)

Negro League Reunion (left to right)
Jim Zapp, Ed Derrick, Doc Dennis, Sidney Bunch, Ed Martin, Sue Bridgeforth, Elliott Coleman,
Taylor Smith, Dan Black, Butch McCord, Henry Kimbro, and James Abernathy (front)
(Courtesy of Hendersonville Links, Inc.)

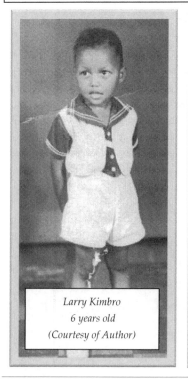

Larry Kimbro
6 years old
(Courtesy of Author)

Tom Wilson
Baltimore Elite Giants Owner
(Courtesy of NoriTech Research, Inc.)

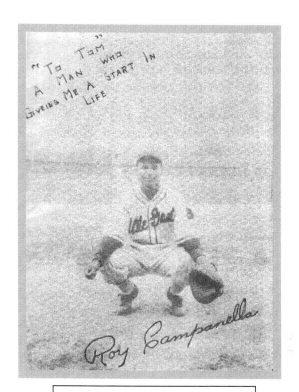

A Young Roy Campanella
(Courtesy of Larry Walker)

Butch McCord
(Courtesy of Author)

CHAPTER 2

Playing Baseball For A Living

"It was one of the best things that ever happened to me, playing baseball for a living," is how my father described the significance of baseball to him. He loved playing it and admitted that he would play it for free, indicating how much he loved it.[1] Throughout his playing career, he meticulously collected pictures and articles documenting his experiences as a player and a fan, and of his life during these times. All the materials in the scrapbook were nicely preserved, in order, as his career progressed.

The scrapbook cover had an Indian chief on the front in full headdress. My father loved western films, so perhaps he selected this cover because an Indian chieftain symbolized the strength and courage Native Americans possessed while facing a hostile America in the 1800s—an aggression similar to the enmity Daddy and all African Americans endured during that time, and certainly what Negro League players faced during his 1937–1953 career.

By the time it got to me, the scrapbook had weathered 60 years and the articles in it flaked at the edges when it was moved even slightly. The pictures themselves were in excellent shape, with notes on the backs of most of them. I often wondered where he stored the scrapbook while we were growing up. When I showed the scrapbook to my stepbrother Larry, he said he never saw it before in his life. Not knowing of the scrapbook's existence until after his death, I wish I'd had the opportunity to discuss its contents with Daddy. For example, there were several articles about Satchel Paige, the greatest pitcher in Negro League Baseball. Seeing the picture reminded me I asked him only once about his thoughts on Satchel Paige. He said, "Satch was an okay guy, man he could throw that ball but I could hit him most times."[2] The way he spoke of Paige led me to believe he had a lot of respect for him as a person and ballplayer, and possibly more stories to share.

My father began his career in the Negro League in 1937 with the Washington Elite Giants. In 1941, on the eve of America's involvement in World War II, he was sent to play for the New York Black Yankees. When I asked him whether he ever considered joining the military during the war, his reply showed another example of his passion for baseball. He wasn't drafted before or during the war; as he put it, his number never came up. His contribution to the war effort was working, during the off-seasons, in the factories that built needed war supplies. He even considered not playing baseball whenever it was time to report to baseball camp; the money was good working at the factories, he said. But he loved playing baseball more, and decided not to give it up.[3]

Daddy played for only one season with the New York Black Yankees before going back to the Baltimore Elite Giants. The scrapbook held an article that highlighted a couple of players who played for the New York Black Yankees. Pictures of players like James Stark, who played first base; John Stanley, a pitcher; Fred "Tex" Burnett, called the "Playing Manager," and my father, who was described as "Shades of Ty Cobb," were included. The manager of the Black Yankees, Fred "Tex" Burnett, changed Daddy from being a lead-off batter to fourth in the lineup. Burnett believed my father could be a consistent home run hitter. Even so, Daddy disagreed with Burnett's assessment of the best position for him in the lineup. When I asked him about this, he said, "I was a good lead-off man that was strong and fast and could hit line drives to get on base. I've always been a lead-off batter, from sandlot ball through my career until I got to New York, and Tex (manager) wanted me to pull that ball over the fence."[4]

Although statistically Daddy didn't hit many home runs in his career, he credited his year with the New York Black Yankees with recognizing his ability to hit home runs.[5] Another positive event happened during his time with the New York Black Yankees: He was selected for his first East-West All-Star Game, which happened in Chicago, Illinois in 1941. An article from the *Chicago Defender* showed a picture of both teams with players standing side by side. My father was second from the left on the East squad in a New York Black Yankees uniform.

When he returned to the Baltimore Elites the next year, he returned to the lead-off batter position. "I went back to where I belonged," is the way he put it to me.[6] But it was a home run hit at Detroit's Briggs Stadium (later known as Tiger Stadium), during a game between the Homestead Grays and the Baltimore Elite Giants during the 1940s, that he often highlighted in his career. The day after that game, it was reported that another player on the team hit the home run, not him. Although he wasn't immediately given the recognition, he took credit for that feat, and I often heard him say, "Whew, I hit a ball out of Briggs Stadium, how did I do that?"[7] The only other ballplayer to do that was Major League Baseball Hall of Famer Ted Williams; he was the first, and regardless of the initial report, Daddy was the second. My father was not a man who boasted about anything he did, but sometimes I wondered if he forgot how many times he told me that story; it came up every time we talked about his baseball career. Looking back, I believe that not getting credit for the Briggs Stadium home run troubled him just as much as his lack of formal education.

In 1997, *USA Today* reported Henry Kimbro of the Baltimore Elites as the second player, black or white, to hit a ball out of Detroit's Tiger Stadium.[8] This made the feat official and at long last validated his claim. As usual, he never told anyone of us of this official documentation. But this was consistent with Daddy living in the present and not in the past.

I was six years old when I first recall my father playing baseball. He had retired from the Negro League and the league had folded, but he still had great passion for the game. By then, he was playing at Hadley Park in Nashville, with a local baseball league. Our family sometimes used these opportunities to have picnics, and of course my brother and I could always play at the park's playground while Daddy played baseball. My mother would sit on a blanket and watch the game from afar.

There was a picture in the scrapbook of my father in his uniform. On one side of him is my brother Phillip, on the other side is me, wearing his hat. I was about six or seven years old, and Phillip a year younger. That picture took me back to when I was clueless of my father's accomplishments. I can say I was aware of one thing, however: my father's exceptional speed. To me, he was the fastest human being alive. I decided this because of a game he played with us after each of his baseball games at Hadley Park. When the game was over, my mother let us run down to the dugout to find Daddy. As we began to walk back, he would say, "I'll race you back to where Mama is."

He'd give us a good head start. Phillip and I would take off running, Phillip always ahead of me, and I remember getting halfway each time when I'd feel this burst of wind pass by me. It was Daddy. At that point I would quit running and throw down my (his) hat, for I hated to finish last. But Daddy was always first, Phillip second, and me bringing up the rear. Adding to my childish indignation, he challenged us by making us believe we had a chance to win. As I look back I laugh about that, because it reminds me of my favorite cartoon character, Charlie Brown, and Lucy tempting him to kick a football, and every time he gave in and attempted to kick it, she'd snatch up the football at the last minute and he'd fall on his back.

At the end of one race, I was so angry about always

losing I started crying. That time, Daddy pulled me over to the side and said, "You never quit, no matter how bad things look. You will beat me one day." Then he smiled and added, "But today is not the day. You just keep trying until that day comes." That lesson would be woven into the person I became.

In his scrapbook were many pictures of him in a baseball uniform: several of him in a Baltimore Elite Giants uniform, and a couple in a Cuban League uniform. There were also two team pictures, one of the 1939 Baltimore Elite Giants championship team and another of the 1949 championship team. Other pictures were of the outfield squad, and of the full team. Most pictures in which he appeared, he was kneeling; in some, he was standing, but in each picture he had the same demeanor, a serious look on his face, his expression reflecting the no-nonsense look I remember of him. Even so, seeing him in those unfamiliar uniforms, it was almost like seeing the pictorial biography of someone I'd never met.

By then I knew he was a passionate player, but, I often wondered what kind of ballplayer he was in his prime. If I'd had the opportunity to watch him play back then, what kind of talent would I have seen during those games?

That first time I saw the scrapbook, and each time I revisited it over the next years, I was taken back to when it came into my possession. A week after the funeral, I went to my mother's house to help her with packing up Daddy's clothes and other items. That's when she gave me the scrapbook. Although I was so eager to immediately begin pouring through it, there wasn't time. My mother wanted to complete the task that day, and I didn't think she could handle waiting another day to go through my father's things. It wasn't easy, but I shifted my focus back to that task, and soon found myself mesmerized by what else I found. Among all the keepsakes was a beautiful men's ring from either the 1939 or the 1949 Baltimore Elite Giants championship team. Just as thrilling, my mother boxed up all of the Negro League books given to my father by family and friends, and gave them to me. In addition, she also gave me all of his Negro League items. When I left the house that day, I felt like a kid who had raided the candy store, and certain that the best candy was the scrapbook.

Excitement eventually gave way to a fear of enormous responsibility. Although my mother didn't say so specifically, it was implied that I was passed a torch of some sort. When I returned to my house, I carefully put the scrapbook in a safe container and told myself to pray about it, and it would come to me what I must do with all of these resources.

The next day after breakfast, I sat in my favorite chair in the living room, both eager and nervous about what I was going to discover. Within the first pages of the scrapbook were several well-preserved photographs and articles, so I began by reading those. Soon, I began to feel like I'd been transported into another time. I could feel the essence of that era, and I could so easily imagine what had come with difficulty before: seeing my dad and the atmosphere of excitement at the baseball park while his games were played. I could hear the upbeat voices of players who, though they might have been shunned and mistreated outside the park, were just happy to be in the moment, playing the game of baseball. It wasn't even a stretch to imagine the crowd's energy during a game. And it seemed I would go on this marvelous trip every time I opened the scrapbook.

Though in more recent times, articles about black players were frequently published in white-owned newspapers, the collection of articles in Daddy's scrapbook had been published by African-American newspapers like the *Chicago Defender, Pittsburg Courier, The New York Amsterdam News,* and others. Article after article detailed him as a player, and gave his team standing in the Negro League and team statistics.

Over the next days, the world around me and the present time seemed to fade away, and I was able to put together a chronology of just how far and wide his career had gone, and the influence it had in promoting the Negro League and cementing his status as a standout player in the league. Most of his time in baseball was with the Elite franchise. He played with the Columbus Elite Giants (1936) and Washington Elite Giants (1937), and when the team moved to Baltimore, Maryland, he played with the Baltimore Elite Giants (1938–1940, 1942–1950). Diversions in his sixteen-year career included one year with the New York Black Yankees (1941), and he finished his career with the Birmingham Black Barons (1951–1953).[9]

It was inspiring to know these things about Daddy, and thanks to all those articles, I was finally able to answer that growing question: What kind of player was he? His baseball resume indicated an exceptionally talented player who was respected in his field, if not always understood by those around him. His batting averages were over .300 during the seasons of 1938, 1941, 1944, 1946, 1947, 1948, 1949, 1950 and 1951, and he played in six Negro League All-Star Games. In 1944 he led the league in stolen bases, and finished only a single home run behind league leaders Josh Gibson and Buck Leonard. In 1945 he tied with a player known as Cool Papa Bell for the league lead-in at-bats. In 1946, he hit .371, led the league in runs scored, and tied for the league lead in doubles. He was also part of both Baltimore Elite Giants championship teams of 1939 and 1949.[10]

Before long, I was on a mission to read and collect everything that described his talent. Having never seen my father play baseball when he was in the Negro League, I began with interviewing Butch McCord, Jim Zapp, and others about the Negro League, and particularly about my father. They all confirmed that he was a good baseball player, and might have had the opportunity to play major league baseball if circumstances were different. Thanks to authors like Brent Kelly, John Holway and others who interviewed many players of the Negro League while they were still alive and well, including my father, their voices can be heard through their personal interviews. These authors' books gave me the opportunity to read other players' opinions of my father as a baseball player.

In Brent Kelly's book, *Voices From the Negro League*, Red Moore's response when asked to name the best players you'd come across in the Negro Baseball League was "Jackie Robinson,...Wild Bill Wright, and Henry Kimbro."[11] Frank Duncan, Jr., reflecting on the question of who were the pure hitters, said, "I'd have to put Josh (Gibson), Bill Wright, Kimbro".[12] When asked who belongs in the National Baseball Hall of Fame, Stanley Glenn stated, "Biz Mackey, Gene Benson, and I'd have to say Henry Kimbro...a lot of people misunderstood Henry. He was quiet and he stayed to himself....I found him a real fine baseball player."[13] Player

Jimmy Dean, who was a pitcher with the Philadelphia Stars, said, "Henry was a hard man to pitch to. He could hit. He was evil but he could hit and field. Joe Black, Junior Gilliam, George Hopkins, all those guys were afraid to talk to him. Don't make a mistake; he'd be on your case. He was a tough act to follow."[14]

In another book by Brent Kelly, *The Negro Leagues Revisited: Conversations with 66 More Baseball Heroes*, Andy Porter stated, "Kimbro came to us (Elite Giants) about 1936 or 37. He was good, fast...Kimbro was a great outfielder...good ballplayer, good hitter."[15] Charles Biot stated, "But I was one of the best outfielders in baseball. Me and Kimbro...I think Kimbro might have made it in the major leagues. He was a fine outfielder."[16] Clinton "Casey" Jones, when asked to name some of the best players he ever saw, recalled, "Henry Kimbro was a good (ballplayer) one too."[17] Nap Gulley commented, "He (Kimbro) wasn't known as a home run hitter, but if you happen to get the ball in the wrong place, you could forget about it because he'd hit the ball out of the ballpark."[18] Wesley "Doc" Dennis, a fellow Nashvillian who knew my father well, stated, "I played with Roy Campanella, Junior Gilliam, and Henry Kimbro. He (Kimbro) was sort of gruff, but he wasn't nasty."[19] William "Sou" Bridgeforth, the last Negro League owner alive until his death in 2004, said, "Our best hitters were Henry Kimbro, Ed Steele, and Pijo King."[20]

Another interesting part of Daddy's baseball career I discovered: He played in the California Winter League, described as America's first integrated professional baseball league, a league that allowed black teams to compete against white teams. According to one author, "Rube Foster, called the Father of Negro League Baseball, brought the first Negro League team to California to compete in the 1910-11 winter league."[21] Daddy played during the 1940–1941 and 1941–42 seasons with the Tom Wilson-sponsored team, the Baltimore Elite Giants. During the 1941–1942 season, he played for the Royal Giants. Statistically he did well, with a batting average of .342 during 1940–41, and a batting average of .400 for the 1941–42 season.[22]

The more I read and heard from others, the more I realized that Daddy's contribution to Negro League Baseball was deserving of a formal accolade granted to the best in baseball. In 2002, I solicited written testimonies from well-respected figures in baseball and in the Nashville community to help nominate my father for induction to the Tennessee Sports Hall of Fame. This brought other accolades to Daddy's career to add to the books and articles that mention him.

In response to my requests, John "Buck" O'Neil wrote in a letter of support to the nominating committee, "Just as your dad was an excellent lead-off hitter in whom we could trust to get the job done ... it would be great if Henry and other Negro Leagues players receive this honor."[23]

Larry Schmittou, former owner of the Nashville Sounds Minor League team, wrote, "In baseball, a truly great player is said to be a five-tool player. The five tools are running, speed, strong throwing arm, able to hit for a high average and superior defensive skills. Henry Kimbro was a five-tool player."[24] Judge Adolpho A. Birch, Jr., the first African-American Supreme Court Justice of Tennessee, stated, "He (Henry Kimbro) was a baseball giant ... in the Old Negro League. As a child, I delighted in watching him play with the likes of Buck Leonard, Josh Gibson and Cool Papa

Bell. He belongs up there with those great sportsmen."[25]

Clinton "Butch" McCord (Baltimore Elite Giant, 1948–1950) said, "Your father and I go a long way back when it comes to Negro Baseball. He was an excellent example of what baseball was all about—modeling, teaching, disciplining, and playing for the love of the game."[26]

Larry Walker, former owner of the Old Negro League Sports Shop of Nashville, wrote, "Henry Kimbro had a most impressive career in the Negro league. ... He had a lifetime batting average of at least .300. He was the 1939 Negro National League batting champion when Josh Gibson, Willie Wells and all the greats were still in the league. As an historian, I am surprised he wasn't inducted (into the Major League Baseball Hall of Fame) before a couple of others that have been."[27]

And finally from the 17th Councilman District of Nashville, Tennessee, Councilman Ronnie Greer stated, "As a native Nashvillian who was an outstanding professional baseball player in Baseball's Negro League ... Mr. Kimbro's exploits are legendary. Mr. Kimbro was a prominent, successful Nashville businessman who owned and operated Bill's Cab Company for more than two decades. Mr. Kimbro's accomplishments are a legacy that will serve as a benchmark for today's youth."[28]

Yet, no sportsman can claim only strengths. In spite of tremendous ability that made him a notable ballplayer in the league, Daddy's weak points were as well known as his strengths. As a player, one weakness was, by his own admission, fielding ground balls in the outfield. In an interview Daddy gave in the *Sports Collector Digest* published March 7, 1997, he said, "I had a bad way with ground balls cause I come up in these parks around here (Nashville) and these rocks and ditches and things."[29] Reading this, I was reminded of him telling me that he saw one of his teammates in the outfield get several of his teeth knocked out because of a bad hop; after that, Daddy was always a little hesitant on ground balls, though he did take great pride in his ability to catch any kind of ball in the outfield.

Another limitation in his game was hitting a knuckle ball. "He hated to hit against a particular pitcher he faced in the Cuban League, major league baseball pitcher Emil 'Dutch' Leonard,"[28] my stepbrother Larry once stated.[30]

Of course, I have also read and heard stories about the Henry Kimbro who was described as a loner, evil, mean, and an unsociable character. Frazier Robinson (Baltimore Elites Giants, 1943, 46–50) wrote a book called *Catching Dreams: My Life in the Negro Baseball League.* In the book, Robinson shared a couple of stories about my father when he got in a slump. He wrote, "If he (Kimbro) was in a slump, he might go out and just get drunk as he can…on top of being angry at the world, he'd be drunk…That's the way he was when he'd get in a slump…you couldn't get close to him. He was a good hitter—he'd won a batting championship down in Cuba."[31]
Jim Zapp, who played with Daddy on the Baltimore Elite Giants team, told me that my father would get in a funk when he wasn't hitting well, but that wasn't often. Zapp also confirmed what Frazier Robinson described in his book: that my father was a man that couldn't hold his liquor well. Zapp shared with me an odd story he heard about my father, that he once drove his car through the downtown arcade in Nashville. The arcade was like an outdoor shopping area covered by a glass roof, and cars weren't allowed to go into

the area. Zapp said he really couldn't tell me what *that* was about, but it was one of those odd stories he remembered being told about my father.[32]

Daddy told me himself that his temper sometimes got the best of him when he was playing. He described how he got so angry with umpires during games when they made bad calls that made him out on a strike, he would break the bat in half. When I asked him why he'd get so angry, he replied, "They (umpires) would call strikes when the ball wasn't even near the plate, and that just made me mad when I was standing there and knew different....I couldn't take that." Later I questioned him on why he broke the bats. He replied, "Because it was better to take it out on the bat, right?"[33]

In Bob Luke's book, *The Baltimore Elite Giants*, Luke documented how my father's temper might have gotten the best of him. He wrote, "The Grays delayed the start of the game for twenty minutes protesting Kimbro's presence in the Elites' lineup. Kimbro had been ejected from a game the previous week against the Stars for starting a fight. Grays officials argued that Kimbro should have also received a suspension, which would have made him ineligible for this game." [34]

Larry, my stepbrother, saw firsthand how Daddy handled tense situations on and off the playing field, and once told me, "Daddy had a short fuse, and there was never any doubt where he stood on things."[35] While stating this, Larry shared a story he was witness to during our father's playing days with the Baltimore Elite Giants. Daddy had brought two fellow ballplayers over to his house in Nashville, and as the evening went on, his teammates did or said something that made him mad. Larry said, "Daddy stood up and bluntly told them they had to get out of his house and get out now."[36] Although they were stunned—it was Daddy who had driven them there!—they got up and left the house, and had to make it to their next destinations on their own.

My father had another talent that was useful during his baseball career. Because of his experience with working in a gas station and transporting bootleg spirits through Tennessee, and his knowledge of car mechanics, he was often called on to help drive the team bus and help with mechanical issues.

Shannon Jones, who was possibly the last living bus driver for a team in the Negro Baseball League at the time I met him, shared stories of Daddy's driving and mechanical talents with me in a 2008 interview. He was a historical treasure I was fortunate to meet through his daughter, Laverne Gray; she and I attend the same church, Patterson Memorial United Methodist Church in Nashville. He and I grew to know each other well, and I came to affectionately call him "Mr. Jones." The first time I met him in church, he eagerly offered that he'd known Daddy well, because they worked together on a baseball team; Mr. Jones was the official bus driver for the Nashville Black Vols, Nashville Cubs and Elite Giants.

Traveling in the Negro League was long and hard at times, Mr. Jones revealed in our interview. Each team had relief drivers they counted on, and who were as important as the regular team driver since they were crucial to achieving sometimes exceedingly long distances to meet their scheduled games. Mr. Jones's relief drivers were Arthur Hefner and Henry Kimbro. Mr. Jones explained that the relief driver had to be a person with experience as a driver, and some mechanical skills also. My father had a reputation of being a good driver who could handle the team bus even in an emergency.[37]

As the relief driver, Daddy helped Mr. Jones drive to some faraway places, like the time they drove to Saskatchewan Province in Canada. Right after playing a game in Huntsville, Alabama, the team headed north to play for three weeks in various Saskatchewan cities like Regina, Indian Head, and others, all within a 200-mile radius. Though the distance was far from home, Mr. Jones said it was an enjoyable experience, one quite different from their games in the United States, which were played in the South during the era of the notorious Jim Crow laws. In Canada, they played against white Canadian teams, and in this part of the world, there were no restrictions on what hotels they could stay at or where they could eat. This freedom of choice and acceptance was repeated whenever they traveled to Canada, and they were always treated well.[38]

Mr. Jones told me one interesting story that reflects the Canadians' respect back then for the talents of the Negro League players. On one of their trips to Canada, they stayed at a hotel by a golf course. One day, player Wesley "Doc" Dennis went out to hit golf balls at the course. A couple of Canadians saw him hitting and inquired about his skills, then asked him to hit a couple of balls. They were so impressed with his playing ability, they invited him to join them as a team member and play with them. My husband, Herbert Hamilton, an avid golfer, confirmed that Doc Dennis had a reputation in the Nashville community as an outstanding golfer.[39]

Of my father, Mr. Jones said, "He was a great ballplayer. He was about business and didn't laugh or play around, but don't cross him if you didn't want trouble, just don't cross him. His nickname for my father was "Cokie."[40] The word came from the color of the most popular soft drink at the time, Coca-Cola. Mr. Jones explained, "Because of your daddy's dark complexion, he looked like he was sweating ink when he played."[41] According to him, Daddy laughed about that; they were good friends with mutual respect for each other.

Near the end of their baseball careers, their paths diverged. When Sou Bridgeforth purchased the Birmingham Black Barons, he merged his Nashville team (formerly the Baltimore Elite Giants) with the Barons in Birmingham, Alabama. Mr. Jones didn't go with Sou Bridgeforth to Birmingham, and instead began to work with the Nashville Police Department. Daddy spent the last three years of his baseball career as a Birmingham Black Baron, as a player and manager according to Mr. Jones.[42] Hearing of his management position didn't surprise me, because Daddy always possessed leadership skills. Despite having a 6th-grade education, he was one of the smartest men I ever knew. I was a witness to these skills as I worked with him in his business as a bookkeeper.

In the winter of 1945, Jack Roosevelt Robinson signed with Branch Rickey's Dodgers organization, and the door to integrate Major League Baseball was unlocked. Even though this led to the slow death of Negro League Baseball, it was an opportunity for the next generations to play professional baseball as equals. My father appreciated what Jackie Robinson accomplished, because he was one of those players who knew he could not have done what Robinson did. He summarized it by saying, "Jackie was not the best player in the Negro Baseball League, but he was the best man for that job. If it was me, somebody would have been in the jail, and somebody would have been under the jail."[43] He was referencing the verbal attacks, physical abuse and negative atmosphere present in Major League Baseball when Jackie joined the Brooklyn Dodgers. Daddy felt he wouldn't have lasted one week under those terrible circumstances.

There is much written about how only select Negro League players were courted by white professional baseball teams once the color barrier line was crossed. For many black players, this meant the end of the Negro Baseball League was the end of their career. For my father, the end of his career came when he decided, "It was time, time to make a living for my family." I am sure if he had a genuine offer to play in Major League Baseball Daddy would have taken it, but no one made an offer. In his book, *The Integration of Baseball in Philadelphia,* Christopher Threston wrote the following on my father.

> "By the time Jackie Robinson broke into professional baseball in 1946, Kimbro was in his mid-thirties and, according to typical major league policy, classified as over the hill. ... In 1946, Kimbro hit for a lusty .376 average against still formidable Negro League competition. The next season, Kimbro continued his fine play by batting .363 and continued his fine play. No major league team took a chance on him. There remains little doubt that a player of

Kimbro's ability could help a major league team."[44]

According to my stepbrother Larry, who was old enough at the time to have memories of this, Daddy remained an exceptional player toward the end of his career. Larry told me that when he was about 11 or 12, when Sou Bridgeforth owned the Nashville Elite Giants, Larry served as a ball boy with the team. They had a game with a white Triple A team, and this team was young and behaved arrogantly playing against the Elites. According to Larry, Daddy told a couple of his teammates to get themselves on base and "He would snatch one out." He did, in fact, snatch one out of the park, and they went on to defeat the Triple A team.[45]

My father had no regrets; he felt fortunate to have the career he had, for it changed his destiny. He said of life, "Everything has its time." His time in baseball over, he kept moving forward, never looking back. To him, his retirement from baseball was simply the beginning of his time for being a businessman, father and grandfather. This, I know, is why there were no discussions with us, his children, about his life as a baseball player. He was about the business of the present, and he was good at that, too.

(Left to Right)
Jim Zapp, Henry Kimbro and Butch McCord
(Courtesy of Larry Walker)

Henry Kimbro (1st from left) with teammates
(Courtesy of Babe Ruth Museum)

Henry Kimbro
(Courtesy of Babe Ruth Museum)

Henry Kimbro after hitting a homerun
(Courtesy of Babe Ruth Museum)

JimZapp and I
(Courtesy of Author)

Mr. Shannon Jones, Jr.
Nashville Stars Baseball Team Bus Driver
(Courtesy of the Shannon Jones Family)

Part of a Baltimore Elite Team Program
(Courtesy of NoirTech Research, Inc.)

Nashville Stars Baseball Club Bus
(Courtesy of the Shannon Jones Family)

Wesley "Doc" Dennis
(Courtesy of Author)

The Baltimore Elite Giants - 1945
(Courtesy of The Negro League Museum)

The Baltimore Elite Giants - 1949
(Courtesy of The Negro League Museum)

CHAPTER 3

The Cuban Connection

If you were opening Daddy's scrapbook, the first item you would see is a picture of Roy Campanella, a former Baltimore Elite Giants player who left Negro League Baseball to play in the Mexican Baseball League. On the picture, he wrote: "To all my teammates on the Elite team. I wish I was there to help our club win the championship this year." During this time, from 1942–1943, Campanella was playing baseball in the Mexican League because he'd had a disagreement with Elite team owner Tom Wilson. Campanella eventually returned to the United States to play with the Baltimore Elites in 1944.[1]

There was a long history of Negro League players playing in Mexico, Cuba, the Dominican Republic and other Latin countries, either during the Negro League's winter seasons, or permanently during the regular baseball seasons. Players could make a lot more money in these leagues than in the United States, and several were recruited to leave the Negro League to play for a higher salary than they could make in the states. As one author put this, "Hundreds of stars from the Negro Leagues played in Latin America from 1908 through the mid-1950s. The money was appealing. In the 1930s, the average Negro League player was earning about $500 a month....The playing schedule was easy...and the fields themselves were lush green and well maintained."[2]

My father played in Cuba during several winter seasons, as did many other professional baseball players, both black and white. Segregation hadn't yet found a place in the Caribbean baseball leagues. Black and white players stayed in the same hotels; they could eat together; and there were no Jim Crow restrictions in Cuba as in the United States. Daddy said it was the first time in his life he felt free to be who he was, and treated like an equal. Even better, the Cuban people were warm and welcoming, and they respected talented ballplayers. Daddy was considered one of the best players during the times he played there. My mother always lit up whenever she talked about those days in Cuba, and about Daddy's status, she simply stated that he was the best, plus he was treated like a superstar. She went on to explain how they called his name during a game, *"Kin—bro, Kin—bro, Kin—bro!"*[3] This is the type of hero worship any player enjoys, and of course that thrilled my mother too.

My father made his debut as a baseball player in the

Cuban League during the fall of 1939, he played with Cum Posey's Homestead Grays.[4] "At the end of the season, the writers began the tradition of selecting an All-Star team, with the best players in each positions based on their performance."[5] He was selected as the best outfielder for that season. During the 1939–40 winter league while playing for the Almendares team; he led the league in stolen bases, with 18 for the season.[6] The team finished first in the league. When he returned to Cuba for the 1947–48 season, he elevated his player status to star player. In the midst of an integrated Cuban League that included some of Major League Baseball's best players, he won the batting title with a .346 batting average and set an all-time record of 104 hits, the most hits by any player in a single season.[8] He was also a member of the vaunted Havana Championship Team.[9] When he played again with the Havana team during the 1948–49 season, he led the league in walks, with 73.[10]

These feats were documented by articles from Cuban newspapers that included pictures of Daddy, in a Havana team baseball uniform, standing with teammate James "Lefty" La Marque, who played for the Kansas City Monarchs, and manager Miguel Gonzales. The Havana team manager, Miguel Gonzales, was a Cuban star who had a long and distinguished career in Major League Baseball. He returned to Cuba and became the foundation of Cuban baseball's growth. All three in the picture were smiling, and it's the best smile I ever saw on my dad. Another picture was his team picture of the 1939–40 Almendares championship squad.

Also in this section were two interesting articles. In one article a photograph is captioned, "Violent collision with

Kimbro" [running to home base] and a catcher [blocking home base]. The result was both players on the ground, the pitcher with the ball looking to throw someone out. The other article showed Daddy coming home to his teammates' congratulations after hitting a home run.

I didn't have to rely completely on other sources to write this account of Daddy's time in Cuba; I had firsthand accounts from my mother. Although Daddy's scrapbook chronicled his accomplishments, my mother's stories were much more entertaining and exciting to hear, and told from a Cuban's perspective. Also, this part of the scrapbook was mostly in Spanish, and I needed her help to interpret it. Surprisingly, I discovered there were more pictures of the island beauty who captured Daddy's heart than pictures of his baseball career in Cuba. That beauty was my mother, his wife of 47 years and business partner, and who served as the guardian of his baseball memorabilia until her death.

Erbia Candida Mendoza Kimbro was born in the city of Esperanza, Cuba. She was born October 7th, 1926 to Phillippe and Justas Mendoza. She grew up with two older brothers as a bit of a free-spirited little girl, encouraged by her father. She often shared stories of her adventures with her brothers in a town surrounded by sugarcane fields. One of the most fascinating tales happened when she and her brothers, Dago and Orlando, got on a train that transported sugarcane. Their purpose was to eat some of the sugarcane on board. When it was time to get off the train, both brothers got off successfully—but there was a problem with her disembarking from the train because it began moving. It took some time for her brothers to successfully get her off the train, resulting in them getting home late. Only the brothers got in trouble with Grandpa Phillippe, because, as he told them, they were responsible for my mother as long as she was with them.[11]

My mother loved her father for allowing her to go out with her brothers during a time (the 1930s) when girls were restricted. Yet as she got older, both her parents had high expectations of her, because she was considered the brightest, boldest and most daring of her siblings. After finishing Esperanza High School, Momma was sent to Havana to attend Teachers College, where she completed her education and earned a Teacher's Certificate. The lady she stayed with was affectionately called Mammayita. She was an old friend of the Mendoza family. An arrangement was made between families for Momma to stay with her and go to school. She spoke of Mammayita as her second mother, she had fond memories of her time spent in her house in Havana.[12]
It was during her college tenure in Havana that she was introduced to my father.

One of my father's Cuban teammates, Lazara Medina, was a friend of Mammayita's family.[13] As my mother tells the story, Daddy was extremely quiet when he first came to call on her; he didn't know a lick of Spanish and she didn't know any English. Their courtship was a classic old world-style romance, the kind you'd see played out on a Hollywood movie set on a tropical island in simpler times. During their dates, they always had a couple of people chaperone them, as was tradition, and to serve as their interpreters. Early in the courtship, their dates included going to the movies, out to eat, and to other events, for which my father paid for everyone in the party, also dictated by tradition. Momma said that Daddy never seemed discouraged by the challenges presented by the chaperones and their added expense; he just kept coming back.[14] My dad's recollection on this was somewhat different, however. Later in the courtship, he told me he "got smart on that deal" of paying for all those people by making the dates simple and inexpensive, like going for ice cream, taking walks on the pier of the beach, and a couple of other free ideas he came up with.[15]

After a long period of courtship and returning to Cuba, Daddy went to Grandpa Phillippe to ask for my mother's hand in marriage. Grandpa said yes, and my parents were married on September 5, 1952, in Nashville, Tennessee. They then immediately flew to Chicago, Illinois for Daddy's game there. The lack of a honeymoon wasn't an issue. As a native-born Cuban, my mother naturally loved the game of baseball, her passion for the game passed on to her by her father. In his youth, her father, Philippe Mendoza, had himself been a player in the Cuban League, and my mother was given a photo by Grandpa Philippe, showing him on a Cuban team in his younger days.[16]

At first I thought the love of baseball Cubans have was a passion that evolved over time, but my mom stated it was more than that. As the story was told to her by her father, baseball was a symbol of Cuban freedom. When the Spaniards ruled Cuba starting in the 1500s, the national sport was bullfighting, and they required Cubans to attend to show their respect for Spain.[17] The Cubans preferred baseball. When the Cuban people acknowledged their preference for baseball over bullfighting, the Spanish rulers banned the playing of baseball in Cuba in 1869. As Cubans struggled for their independence from Spain, baseball steadily grew and became organized in the 1870s, although baseball was still banned by the Spanish rulers. It was not until the end of the Spanish-American War in 1898 that Cuba became free of Spain's rule. An interesting aside: In the early 1900s, way ahead of the United States, black players were allowed to play in the Cuban League.[18] My mother shared her passion for baseball with my father. I can remember our television at home playing nothing but Major League Baseball games on the weekends. And when we were fortunate enough to have two televisions, we had two different major league games playing at the same time. Growing up, that was when I had my best naps. I remember my parents' conversations about the baseball players from each team, especially if they were African Americans or Cubans. My mother was a walking library of baseball, my father the strategic coach of the game.

In much the same way, my parents were true partners during their marriage. Just as they had long conversations about baseball, they had deep discussions about my father's business dealings. My mother was Daddy's conscience in dealing with every kind of problem, in fact, especially in dealing with my brother and me. My mother loved my father, and often described him as a man with a good heart, further belying some others' perceptions of him as "evil" or mean. She understood him better than anybody did. Momma was proud of Daddy as the baseball player, businessman, father and husband, with deep respect for him as a man who accomplished so much, and her respect grew even more when she saw firsthand the racism that existed in this country that posed additional challenges to Daddy throughout his life.

My mother also experienced racism from both the white and black community in her new home. Growing up in the South, I had learned early what racism was, and that it was more painful when you experienced it from persons who look like you. I remember as a child, we all were at a family gathering, and like any child I roamed around the place with the other kids. As I came near my mother, who was walking toward me, I heard two women, relatives of ours, make comments about how my mother had no business leaving her country to marry my dad. I hurt for her, because I knew she had heard them. My reaction was similar to what my dad's would have been; I put the meanest frown I could on my face and stopped to stare at those women. But my mother seemed more worried about how I felt than about the effect those women's words had on her. Instead of acknowledging their statement, she picked me up and said, "Let's go get some chocolate cake." She knew I loved chocolate anything. I still do.

As a devout Catholic, Momma was a woman of God, and the most gracious Christian I knew; she saw good in everybody, the complete opposite of my father that way. My mother and I had another special bond: like my father, even as a child I felt I had to protect her. Because she struggled with the English language for so many years, I would come home from elementary school and teach her what I learned in English that day. That time we spent as teacher and student in reverse roles is the memory I hold dearest, because no one knew about it; it was just between my mom and me. We had fun, and I know this is why I went on to become an educator. Yet she was my first and best teacher, since she taught me how to be a good student and showed me skills I needed to be successful in school. I never wanted her to ever be disappointed in me, just proud. I hope she was.

Yet there wasn't much I could do about the racial prejudice she faced. When my parents went to events or were out and about in the city, no one ever dared cross the line with us because my father was exceedingly protective of my mother, my brother and me. His demeanor was of an on-duty guard who would strike if threatened. But Daddy couldn't be with us all the time, and during those moments, like the one at the family gathering, Momma faced the ugliness of racism. She was always gracious and had a quiet strength that frustrated me, until I discovered that she was the strongest of us all. It was her silent inner strength and character of steel that my father drew strength from, and from which he learned how to better deal with people. My mother's greatest influence on my dad made him a better person and father, and a polished and successful businessman.

Because of my mother, Phillip and I learned that the world was a much bigger place beyond our house on Joyner Avenue in Nashville. Most summers when we were little, we traveled to Cuba to visit our grandparents. I remember going to Cuba and spending time with my grandparents, aunts and uncles. Since I was the first grandchild born in my mother's family, and my brother a year later, we got a lot of attention from the family in Cuba. My fondest memory is from when I was in the Havana airport waiting for our grandfather, Phillippe Mendoza, to come pick us up. I didn't yet know who he was, so I anticipated every old man coming toward us as my grandfather, *except* this tall elderly man who hid behind a pillar close to us and peeked out occasionally. I was scared of this man, and wanted my grandfather to hurry and come pick us up. I pointed this character out to Momma, and she jumped up with delight and went to hug him; he was our grandpa. Needless to say I didn't like him at first, just because of that experience. But it didn't take long for my brother and me to adore him. Both my grandparents in fact, Phillippe and Justas Mendoza, were wonderful grandparents who loved us very much even though they never learned to speak English. This is how I learned that love and a true heart transcend any language barrier.

Cuba was a wonderful place for a child to visit. The island had a warm sun and a gentle breeze each time we visited. My brother and I would go to the sugarcane field where we tasted sugarcane and ran freely. Another experience I still remember was with my aunts and other family members. It was an event for them to get me ready each day and do my hair. We visited everybody in the town that they knew, I guess to show us off. You might have said my brother and I were celebrities, because in each introduction, I always heard "Kimbro's children." He was still considered a Cuban superstar long after he played baseball.

I was raised on Cuban food, which I love more than soul food. Every kind of rice, black beans, fried bananas, arroz con pollo, and paella are still my favorite foods. One visit, our grandfather included us in helping him get a pig in the backyard ready to be dinner, but things went haywire when the pig got away from him and ran all over the yard squealing while Phillip and I were screaming and running away from it. The pig ran into the house, and at one point I saw everybody in the house come out screaming and running into the yard, too. Grandfather finally captured the pig, and it became one of the greatest meals I ever had.

These types of memories endeared the Cuban culture

to me because I was part of the experience of being Cuban the many times we visited the island. I loved listening to Afro-Cuban music when my mother's family would all dance most evenings after dinner. I still find myself dancing today to that music whenever I hear it; it takes me back to my grandparent's living room.

But as good as I felt about the Cuban culture, Cuba's politics was a sore issue with my mother's family. That was when I saw emotions and behaviors get raw and aggressive, especially my grandfather's. He was quite vocal about Cuba and the direction it was going under its leader at the time, Fulgencio Batista. In the early 1950s, Batista's government was in power but it was felt he was more interested in serving the United States' interest than the Cuban interest. On those visits, I recall the name "Batista" being mentioned several times in angry and loud conversations. In 1956, the Batista government was overthrown by Fidel Castro during his revolution movement. Emotions were even worse then, because of the communist undertone at that time. We were unable even to visit Cuba after that because of the political climate. My mother's immediate family began to get out of Cuba, with my grandparents the last to leave. There was concern that my grandfather's vocal opposition to the Castro's government would land him in jail or worse, but eventually they were allowed to leave and come to the United States, never to return.

My favorite cousin, Mario Aguilar Jr., described to me how hard life was in Cuba after Castro came to power. His own father was sent to a work camp and they were thrown out of their house. When Mario was eight, his family was able to leave Cuba and go to New York.[19] My favorite aunt and also my godmother, Merida Mendoza, along with my mother-the first family member to come to the United States-helped sponsor other family members' immigration to the United States. Today my Cousin Mario's family owns a successful Cuban restaurant in Tampa, Florida, formerly called La Ideal and later called the Aguilar. Every time I visit my sister Maria, who lives in St. Petersburg, Florida, we visit their restaurant, and each visit takes me back to my grandparents' house in Cuba and my mother's cooking.

When Americans could no longer travel to Cuba, we started visiting New York City—by that time, most of Momma's family was living there. Each summer, we had great experiences like going to Rockefeller Center, the Empire State Building, the New York Mets games, and other events and sites.

One of our visits to New York was a unique experience. We were taken to a section of New York to meet someone. When my mother, Phillip and I arrived, there was an old man sitting in a wheelchair, and I recall he had the biggest grin on his face. Phillip and I were introduced as "Kimbro's kids." He shook our hands and let out a chuckle. I didn't recognize his name at the time, but today I'm amazed that we met the great Roy Campanella that day. Roy Campanella played with our dad on the Baltimore Elite Giants team, went on to star in Major League Baseball, and was inducted into the Major League Baseball Hall of Fame. I had no clue at the time who he was, but now that meeting is a treasured memory.

There were many such memories with my mother, and of the chapters in this book, this was the hardest to write, but also the most rewarding; Momma was the foundation of our family, a willing unsung hero who always put God first, her family second, and herself last. While writing this, I went through several boxes of tissues but they were happy tears too. In remembering her and my father, it reminded me of the special life they shared together and the incredible gift I was given in having them as my parents. When my father passed, I cried because of the loss to our family, but I am always comforted in hearing his voice saying, *Don't carry on about me, it was just my time.* When my mother passed I was devastated, and I still miss her so much. Though I've learned to live with her loss, there will always be a hole in my heart that will never repair itself.

There is a passage in the bible, Philippians 4:13 (KJV), that states, "I can do all things through Christ, who strengthens me." As a Christian, I know that God blessed my mother with the power to achieve the improbable connection of a Cuban woman and African-American man, worlds apart, to find each other, build a family, and experience timeless and unconditional love. My mother would always say, "If it is in God's will." That's the type of faith that taught me what a mighty God we serve. Their "Cuban connection" is a testament to God's glory; their union surely was part of God's plan.

Left to Right
Negro League Player J. Lamarque, Manager M. Gonzalez & Henry Kimbro
(Courtesy of Author)

Daddy's Championship Team in Cuba
(Courtesy of Author)

Mom's Friends (Second to Right)
(Courtesy of Author)

Grandma & Grandpa Mendoza
(Courtesy of Author)

Grandpa Mendoza's Baseball Team (Second from right standing)
(Courtesy of Author)

Erbia C. Mendoza (Mom)
(Courtesy of Author)

Mom & Mammayita
(Courtesy of Author)

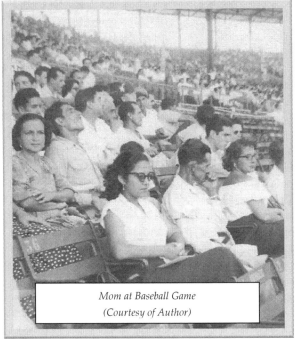

Mom at Baseball Game
(Courtesy of Author)

Mom in Havana, Cuba
(Courtesy of Author)

Mom, Phillip and I in Cuba
(Courtesy of Author)

CHAPTER 4

Life After Baseball

When I came along in my father's life, he was at the end of his career. In fact, the year I was born, 1953, was the year he retired from Negro League Baseball (Birmingham Black Barons). I would like to think he retired because of me but I'm sure there were other factors, like the fact that, by then, the Negro League was on a downward slide in trying to survive.

When he retired, Daddy returned to Nashville, Tennessee. While in the Negro League, he drove a cab for a taxi company during the baseball off-seasons. When he retired from baseball, he made his living driving his own car as a cab at Bill's Cab Company. After a couple of years he bought Bill's Cab Company, and ran it successfully for twenty-two years until he sold it and retired.

My memories of my father are many and rich, traversing many emotions. Growing up, he was more "my father" than "Daddy" to me. As I became an adult, he was more of a daddy to me than a father. As a father, he was a strict disciplinarian, breadwinner, and ruler of the nest. Every decision for the family began and ended with him. As my father, he was my protector, director, and supporter as well. As a disciplinarian he was hard but fair, unyielding but rational, adamant but sensible. My siblings share my views, but as his children, we each had our own unique relationship with him. One thing we all had in common is that we were all important to him and he loved us.

So many moments define who my father was to me. He didn't tolerate disobedience of any kind, and we all knew that. Growing up, we learned how to be respectful and obedient or we would suffer the consequences. And I was obedient, most of the time.

My brother Phillip and I were playing in a neighborhood baseball game. My mother told us we could play until she called us for dinner, and then we had to come straight home. After playing for a while, we heard my mother call, and we called back, saying, "Here we come!" But we continued to play and let time get away from us. The next sound we heard was the back door being kicked. I was at bat, and I immediately dropped the bat, screaming, "We coming Daddy, we coming Daddy!" Phillip was already ahead of me, screaming the same thing.

When we got there I expected to get a whipping, but in sight of the kids playing the game with us—all of whom had stopped to watch what would happen—Daddy just grumbled at us for not responding to our mother when she called. We were escorted into the house and told to wash up and go eat dinner.

There are two memories that are most endearing to me. The first occasion happened the Halloween I was in the third grade. The year before, I played a mouse in a school play and had a full costume. I hated that costume: it was hot, and I could barely see out of the mask. Yet it became my Halloween costume for two years running, with the neighborhood kids calling me "Rat Girl." And of course I was embarrassed.

Halloween night, while we were going from house to house to trick or treat, everybody in my group started to run, to cover more houses in the time we had left. Because I couldn't see well out of the mask, I didn't see a ditch, and fell hard into it. I laid there and cried for what seemed like forever, until I felt arms lift me up with ease. I kept crying even when I saw my father's face. I remember crying and thinking at the same time, *it's my daddy come to rescue me, everything is going to be okay, even in this awful rat suit.*

That night, Daddy was my hero. He didn't say a word; just let me go on while he carried me home. By the time we got to the house, I had stopped crying and fallen to sleep. The next day, my mother informed me that Daddy told her to get rid of the rat suit. He made a decision that I would have another costume next year. She also added he couldn't take his little girls agony. As I can remember, my dad displayed compassion on my behalf several times.

On another occasion, I was in middle school. A boy in my class kept pulling my pigtails. I told the boy to stop or I would make him sorry. During this period in my life, I'd already gotten in trouble for losing my cool a couple of times, and had already made one trip to the principal's office for an altercation of some kind. My mother warned me the next time I was sent to the office, my father would "handle it." This wasn't on my mind the next time the boy pulled my hair, and I pushed him over the classroom chairs. When he got up, we started to fight, until the teacher corralled both of us and took us to the principal's office. But of course I recalled my mother's warning by the time the school called to inform my parents of my misdeed.

When my father got home, I was prepared for an unpleasant punishment. But instead of getting the worst, he called me to the kitchen, where we often received our punishments, asked me to sit down, and calmly told me that I was a young lady now, and fighting was not acceptable. "You know you're smarter than the average bear," he said, which is a statement that came from a Yogi Bear cartoon we use to watch. He went on to say, "I challenge you to start using your brain power. If you're as smart as I think you are, you will outsmart or out-think anybody in any situation."

He went on to share how he could have handled some situations differently in his own life, but as he put it, "I did what I did with what I had, but you have more of an opportunity than I did."

After the shock of seeing his calm, and hearing his vision for me, I decided to take the challenge. I later learned that my mom had told him to help me understand why my behavior wasn't acceptable for my future. In fact, I grew up watching both parents handle various situations in their lives, and knew from an early age that my mother and my father were two different people in that regard. In reflection, I see these differences as a blessing, because I have a combination of both of their styles as part of who I am.

Yet my parents' individual styles adapted to the situation, and needs of each child. With Geraldine, his first daughter, Daddy wasn't involved in any aspect of her life and that brought on a guilt that he carried to his grave. When Phillip and I came along he was a Warden. By the time my younger sister Maria, his last child, came along, he had mellowed out.

Of all of his children, Maria looked more like his mother than any of us, with many of her facial and physical features. She was the baby, and the baby girl, and he doted on and spoiled her. Every day when he came home from work, Maria would sit with him, and they had long conversations about what went on in school, and he listened and sometimes laughed at her stories. He loved and took great pride in all of his children, but Maria was his heart, and she knew it. During this time, my mother became more of the disciplinarian with her than he was.

Maria and Phillip both inherited our father's athletic talent. Both were outstanding athletes in high school, both scholarship athletes in college. Phillip played football, basketball and baseball at Glencliff High School, but was outstanding in every sport. He was a starter for Glencliff High School's baseball team when they won the Tennessee State Baseball Championships, and went to Fisk University on a football and baseball scholarship. Exceptional at baseball like our father, Phillip received an invitation to try out for the Cincinnati Reds Baseball Organization. Maria's career was similar. She was an athletic standout at Father Ryan High

School on the volleyball team and especially on the tennis team, where she won the high school district's tennis championship. She went on to Florida A&M University on an athletic scholarship and won several MEAC conference tennis championships.

Though I played at Fisk University on the first women's volleyball and basketball teams, I was more known for my coaching and athletic administrative achievements, but particularly in the area of coaching, where I excelled. After graduating from Florida State University, I started the women's basketball program at Bethune-Cookman College after being hired there as a teacher. My teams had success every season between 1976 and 1979, even winning a championship. When I was recruited to coach at my alma mater, Fisk University, my players and I gave the school its first championship teams in volleyball and basketball. In 1986, I became the first African-American female athletic director at an NCAA Division III institution.

I often wondered how coaching came so natural to me. I was sure that growing up and playing sports in the neighborhood helped, but when I began to research my father's background, I learned that my knack also had a lot to do with my father, who had served as a coach and baseball manager for the Baltimore Elites and the Birmingham Black Barons. Several former players told me he was good at that too.

Yet there was more to the answer. Learning that Daddy also had an aptitude for coaching, I recalled how he always included me in backyard sessions when he gave my brother instructions on catching and throwing a baseball. In teaching my students, I often praise my dad for promoting my love of playing sports regardless of being a girl. In doing that, he was promoting me, the person who had the opportunity to be whoever I wanted to be. He was ahead of his time with the issue of gender equity, and both my sister Maria and I benefited from it.

Though I was always eager to join him and my brother in those backyard sessions, I always struggled because I was left handed, and he only had right-handed gloves. One day he came home and told us, "Let's go in the backyard to catch and throw." Out of his equipment bag came an old glove, and he called me over and gave it to me. I put it on my left hand, but it wasn't fitting. Daddy walked toward me, saying, "This glove is for you, it's for left-handed ballplayers."

You'd have thought he had given me a brand-new bike. Rather than simply a glove, I felt I was given a key that opened up the door to a special place to which only I was invited.

In fact, both my parents were a big part of my feeling that way during my career. I received many accolades and awards, but they were most proud when I received an appreciation plaque from the 1984 United States Olympic Gold Medal Women's Basketball Team, thanking me for my contribution to their success. My mother, seeing the plaque, stated, "Oh this is so nice," but my father took a long look at the plaque, and then looked at me and said, "Well, isn't this something." I replied to my dad, whose face was lit up with pride, "Yeah, Daddy, this is something." He knew that he and my mother were directly responsible for that accomplishment, one that began with that old left-handed glove that led me to the special place where I'd found myself.

Recently my mentor, Coach John Martin, former Athletic Director at Fisk University, shared a story with me. He told me that during the period when the school's heat was shut down, my dad-who owned a gas station-donated fuel to keep the gymnasium warm. First I was shocked; later, in a quiet moment to myself, I cried remembering my dad as my hero again during a time of struggle in my life. And once again he never said a word.

My brother Phillip, in reflecting on his relationship with Daddy, also saw him as more his father than his daddy, only in his case Daddy remained his father until the end. Phillip shared with me a memory that stood out during his childhood. Our parents bought him a brand-new bike that he admitted to me cost $300. My brother's bike was the envy of the neighborhood kids, and me, because I myself had a recycled hand-me-down bike from the next-door neighbors. One day, Phillip and Wayne Rucker (Phillip's buddy and our next-door neighbor) decided to ride their bikes to 100 Oak Mall, which was five miles from our house. Of course both of their bikes were stolen.[1]

When our father got Phillip home, he was so angry that Phillip received two whippings. When Daddy went into his room for the third time, Phillip thought he was getting a third whipping, but he didn't. Instead, Phillip said Daddy sat down and explained three reasons he'd been angry enough to whip him twice. The first reason, Daddy explained, was that Phillip had broken the rule of leaving the neighborhood, and that put Phillip in a dangerous position. The second reason was he was irresponsible in not securing his bike at the mall, because our parents sacrificed $300 to buy him one of the best bikes, one that would have lasted him a very long time, had it not been stolen. The third reason was that his judgment was stupid, and in the same way Daddy once challenged me to be better behaved, he challenged Phillip to stop making bad judgments.[2]

And similar to what I experienced, Phillip expressed that this talk was a wakeup call for him to stop making poor choices that would put him at risk of getting this kind of punishment again.[3]

Most of the trouble Phillip and I found ourselves in, we found our way out of most of the time. And although Phillip and I are only one year apart in age, Phillip did get punished a lot more than I did. There was also an imbalance in the type of attention Phillip got from our father. After listening to Larry, Phillip and Maria, I can honestly say that my father was harder on Phillip than any of us. This was probably due to Phillip being the son in a time where circumstances allowed Daddy more involvement in raising him. Because of our father's baseball traveling schedule, Larry was raised by Grandma Sallie, with help from Aunt Louise. Though more involved in the lives of his younger three children, with our father's seven-day-a-week, sunup-to-sundown work schedule at his taxicab business to support us, he worked hard and wasn't home much. I can't remember him ever missing a day from work when we were growing up. My mother didn't work, so she would let him know when we got in trouble and needed his attention. While we always got his attention on *that* note, he rarely was available to come to my brother's athletic events, my recitals, and other positive events in which we were involved.

We both now understand that he was busy providing for his family financially, and he did that well. But Daddy always made time to attend one event: our graduations from high school and college. Our parents were strong driving forces in making us understand that getting an education was a top priority in our lives. Due to Daddy's experiences in education, he was determined that every one of us had the opportunity to achieve the education of which he'd been deprived. In particular, he instilled in Larry, Phillip, Maria and me the expectation that we would all get a college education.

In fact, I was the first to get his unusual lesson in the importance of education. While I attended the seventh grade at Cameron High School, he would come by to pick me up for my piano lessons with Ms. Alice McKeever, two miles from the school. After my lesson, he had to go by his cab station that was located on 12th and Jo Johnson Street, to take care of business before taking me home. Each time, he drove through the housing projects and gave me the same speech: "Look at those women with all those children; they get money from the government. This is where you're going to be if you don't get all the education you can get." Each time we drove by, my eyes could barely see over the window of the car, partly because I wasn't tall enough to fully see over the door, but also because it scared me not knowing what I would see each time.

His tactics were hard, but he was always direct and to the point. That exposure to that type of social situation was in my psyche as I grew up; to know that I was going to get an education and, as Daddy would state it, "Get all the education you can get." I always strived to keep going to school even when I wasn't convinced to do so; I felt driven, and couldn't quit if I wanted to. Daddy gave Larry, Phillip,

Maria and me the directive of going to college. Throughout high school, we knew we had to take college prep classes. So when we had to transfer due to integration, we assumed our guidance counselor would support us. That was not my experience when I got to Glencliff High School. My counselor met with me to explain that my dream of college was unrealistic and I would do better going to hair school. I went home and told my dad what she said. I didn't even finish the whole story before he jumped up in a rage, got in his car, and drove off. When I arrived in school the next day, I had several counselors waiting to give me a new schedule that included honors English, Geometry, Chemistry, and other college prep classes. It wasn't until later in the year my new counselor shared what happened. My father drove to school and made the biggest stink they have ever experienced from a parent. Needless to say, I had all the necessary courses needed to go to Fisk University and graduate, and so did Phillip.

I remember wanting to leave Florida State University the first semester I was there to pursue my master's degree. I called home to tell my mother I wanted to transfer to another school because this program was tough academically, but Daddy answered the phone instead. I explained to him I thought it best if I transferred to another school closer to home.

Daddy asked me two questions. One was, "Do you think you can handle the work at this school?" I replied yes. He then asked me, "Are they putting you out of school?" To which I replied, "Of course not." He said, "Then stay there," and hung up the phone.

I remember wishing my mother had answered the phone that day, but today I thank God she didn't. Florida

State University was a rewarding educational experience for me. Two professors, Dr. Billie Jones and Dr. Janet Wells, took me under their wings and helped me appreciate research and writing. They especially encouraged me to research African-American issues; they planted the seed that is the foundation of my passion for telling Daddy's story.

I have many wonderful memories of Daddy, the family man. One of our common family outings was taking a drive to the airport, parking near the runway and just watching the airplanes take off and land. We would talk about where each plane was going, and my mother added this game: if we named a city, she'd ask what state that city was in, or if we named the state, she'd ask for the name of a city in that state. This outing gave me the sense that the world was a much bigger place than 312 Joyner Avenue, where we lived. Added to growing up with our trips to Cuba and the possibilities of other adventures awaiting us, it excited me to imagine where I would travel in the future. Both parents gave us such a gift of the global perspective; one I've tried to give to my son Patrick.

Another family outing that didn't cost a thing, but was priceless was going fishing. Daddy would get a couple of fishing poles and drive to a remote place I'd never seen before, and Phillip, Daddy and I just sat and fished. Daddy taught Phillip more about fishing than me, because I was more interested in keeping the critters off me than anything else!

The most touching moment I recall between my father and me, and one that illustrates that his parenting style adapted even in our adulthoods, occurred when I was much older. At the age of 42, I was diagnosed with breast cancer. I was too scared to tell my parents because I knew the news would hurt them, and I couldn't face the pain this would cause them. I asked my sister-in-law, Demetrius Kimbro, to tell them, and I don't know to this day what their response was. When they were around me they acted normal, as if they knew I couldn't handle seeing them in pain because of me. Being able to handle that situation became less horrible because of that dynamic.

Although this veneer of normality was easier on me, there were moments when I had them reaching out to me. When I had surgery to remove the cancer, Daddy sent me a dozen red roses at the hospital. He did that one other time, when I gave birth to my son Patrick. Both times, the roses brought me joy. My mother insisted on driving me to every chemotherapy trip. That lasted only until the first trip to the oncologist clinic, however. After my first round of treatment, in the car for the drive home, she turned left and almost ran the car into a telephone pole on my side of the car. She'd tried so hard to act normal, but I knew the situation was too much for her.

After the near miss, I joked with her, "Mom, I'm going to survive the treatment, but will I survive the trip home?" She laughed and agreed to my request to have my husband Herb drive me home. She never knew that I told a white lie about that. He couldn't drive me home, because his work hours would dictate I'd have to change my treatment time. So Momma never knew I drove myself to and from each treatment, because knowing that would have caused her pain.

My sister Maria later told me, after she got Dad's "medical book" after he passed away, that every medical problem I'd had was highlighted and tabbed in his book. I then realized how much he'd wanted to talk to me; my father was a man who educated himself on things he didn't know. I admired his tenacity, intelligence and no-nonsense demeanor in pursuing information even if he didn't want to ask me for it.

One of the roles Daddy truly shined in was as grandfather. I once heard comedian Bill Cosby joke about how his parents were such different people as grandparents, he asked the question, "Who are you people?" I found myself asking the same question about my father when he was around my son Patrick—who he insisted on calling "Pat-er-ick," never Patrick—and Phillip's daughters Brooke and Crystal. My stepbrother Larry had three children Sharisse, Sean, and, Alecia. And although Daddy didn't see them much as they were growing up because of location, they were not far from his thoughts. When I was looking through the scrapbook, I found a picture of Larry's kids when they were younger. Although it was the only picture of them he had, it was placed in the front of the scrapbook in a special place.

When Brooke was born, Daddy was beaming with a bright smile that stayed around a long time. The look in his eyes was pure love. There wasn't any agenda of being a father figure, but a jubilant admirer. When Patrick came along it was the same thing; he was on Patrick's every word and action with joyous glee. But with Crystal, as with my sister Maria, Daddy insisted that she reminded him of his mother, Grandma Sallie. Toward the last years of his life, he became obsessed with finding his mother's gravesite in Chapel Hill, Tennessee. He would make the thirty-minute drive there quite often to look for her resting place, but never found it. He remained adamant about Crystal reminding him of

Grandma Sallie, and his emotions were quite open with Crystal. He was overly attentive with Crystal too, more so than with the other two grandchildren.

Daddy's demeanor went to a much more relaxed level with all his grandchildren. Perhaps it was because he finally could let go of the roles of protector, disciplinarian, breadwinner, and ruler of the nest he felt he had to maintain with his children. Or maybe he took pride in knowing that Phillip, Larry, and I had learned well, and he was at peace that his grandchildren were in good hands.

In reflection, Daddy would have been impressed with the next generation of Kimbros. They are outstanding athletes, scholars, a lawyer, teachers, administrators, coaches, businessman, businesswoman and others. He may not have been aware of most of their accomplishments before he died but he would have been impressed with schools like the University of Michigan, Stillman College, Arizona State University, Tennessee State University, and University of Memphis. The seed of education was placed in the hearts of Daddy's children and became rooted in their families to produce the next generation of the best and the brightest from one's man dream.

Daddy and Maria
(Courtesy of Author)

My Parents with granddaughter Brooke
(Courtesy of Author)

My Parents at the Nashville Airport
(Courtesy of Author)

Daddy with Phillip and I
(Courtesy of Author)

*Left to Right
Coach Wayne Moore, Fernando Fox, Phillip Kimbro,
and Coach Leon Moore of Fisk University
(Courtesy of Author)*

*Patrick Hamilton
Glencliff High School
(Courtesy of Author)*

*Phillip Kimbro
Glencliff High School
(Courtesy of Author)*

UNIVERSITY OF MICHIGAN
School of Law
"Senior Day" - May 15, 1993

Daddy's Granddaughter Sharisse
(Courtesy of Carolyn Kimbro)

ARIZONA STATE UNIVERSITY
College of Education
December 16, 2005

Daddy's Granddaughter Alecia
(Courtesy of Carolyn Kimbro)

Daddy's Grandson
Dr. Sean Kimbro
(Courtesy of Author)

Larry and Carolyn Kimbro
(Courtesy of Carolyn Kimbro)

Daddy's Granddaughter Brooke
(Courtesy of Author)

Daddy's Grandson Patrick
(Courtesy of Author)

Daddy's Granddaughter Crystal
(Courtesy of Author)

*Larry's Children
Sharisse, Sean, and Alecia
(Courtesy of Author)*

*Left to Right
Daddy, Maria, Me, and Phillip
(Courtesy of Author)*

The Kimbro Family Gathering with
Daddy's Great Granddaughter Jada
(Courtesy of Demetria Kimbro)

CHAPTER 5

When Glory Calls

This final part of the scrapbook is my favorite section because I was able to write the final entry: of my father being honored at the 1993 Major League Baseball All-Star Game; being posthumously inducted into the 2004 Tennessee State Sports Hall of Fame; being inducted into the Metropolitan Nashville Public School Sports Hall of Fame; being recognized by the National Association of Black Journalists; and becoming a candidate for the Major League Baseball Hall of Fame. He would have been proud of having come from such humble and hard beginnings to be recognized in these ways, especially by the school system he desperately wanted to continue his education with, but wasn't able to, and his home state of Tennessee honor. Even though he wasn't alive for either of the inductions, I felt him in my soul and he was exceedingly connected to the spirit of each of the events. I was so grateful that, before he passed, he was able to live to enjoy some of the honors and events celebrating Negro League Baseball.

When Daddy finally retired from the taxicab business, he came home. His days were spent reading, watching movies, and going to The Old Negro League Sports Shop in Nashville. He spent most evenings there, with other former Negro League players. When I asked, "What are you doing down there?" he usually said, "Just shucking and jiving." The owner of the shop, Larry Walker, told me my dad was more like a grandfather figure, because he gave him a lot of wisdom. In truth, Butch McCord, Jim Zapp, Sou Bridgeforth, Sidney Bunch, and Daddy would share stories and remember when. This meeting place became a feature story in *Sports Illustrated* with several local news media carrying the story. Baseball fans across the country would travel to this tiny shop on Jefferson Street in North Nashville to get autographs and get first hand stories from these guys. This was Daddy's hangout place; my father loved every minute spent there.

Daddy also began to enjoy the accomplishments of his baseball career for the first time in his life; his reflections on his career didn't start until after he retired-reflections fueled by the many books about him in the Negro League that were collected over the years. My father loved to read, and he had the time now to read through all his books. When Negro League history was rediscovered, those players still alive were sought after for interviews, for events honoring Negro League players, and for being a part of history that was hidden in the shadows for so long, especially players like Daddy who were considered stars of the league. In his scrapbook was a copy of a July 6, 1992 *Sports Illustrated* in which he delighted in reading again and again. The article named "Remembering Their Game" featured Negro League players Jimmie Crutchfield, Leon Day, Garnett Blair, John "Buck" O'Neil, Bill Wright, Jim Lamarque, Ted "Double Duty" Radcliffe, Walter "Buck" Leonard, Willie Grace, and Daddy. He signed his copy of the magazine with "To my grandson Patrick, H. Kimbro grandpa."

During his retirement, my father, with my mom accompanying him, was invited to several Major League Baseball team events that honored Negro League players. The Atlanta Braves, Milwaukee Brewers, and Baltimore Orioles are a few of the baseball organizations that sponsored high-profile honors Daddy attended. The driving force behind him going was my mother, however. If left up to my father, he would not have attended. His response to these invitations would have been one of his favorite sayings, "The past is the past, and it is all said and done." But Momma and her adventurous spirit would not be denied the excitement of being around baseball history, and she knew Daddy would enjoy those last hoorahs too.

Once my parents began going on these trips, they really enjoyed it. I remember going to the airport along with my husband Herb, my sister Maria, and her husband Don, to pick up my parents upon their return from attending the Milwaukee Brewers Baseball event. The June 19, 1998 event was where the Milwaukee Brewers Baseball organization honored Daddy by inducting him into the Yesterday's Negro League Baseball Players Wall of Fame, along with other

Negro League stars like Rodolfo "Rudy" Fernandez (1932–1943), Willie Grace (1942–1951), Napoleon "Nap" Gulley (1940 –1950), Albert "Buster" Haywood (1935–1941), Casey Jones (1918–1949), Lester Lockett (1944–1949), Art (Superman) Pennington (1940–1956), and Andrew Porter (1932–1949). After the event, Daddy talked about how the Brewers' organization was a first-class group and how this was done each year with other Negro League players. He accepted how special this was for those players being recognized, so people would learn about the Negro League and the significance of what they accomplished.[1]

My favorite Negro League event had happened five years earlier. My parents, my son Patrick-nine years old at the time-and I attended the 1993 Major League All-Star Game at Camden Yards in Baltimore, Maryland. At this All-Star Game, Negro League players were being honored in a week full of events, with the concluding event being the players' introductions before the start of the All-Star Game. They each wore a replica of their Negro League uniform, from the hats down to their shoes. I loaned the entire outfit to the Tennessee Sports Hall of Fame, with the exception of the shoes-they were stolen after the event in Baltimore.

The 1993 Baseball All-Star Game was so special because my son Patrick was able to share it with his grandpa. My father loved that Patrick was there. Unlike his much earlier reluctance to talk about it with me, for the first time, Daddy initiated the conversation with Patrick about him playing in Negro League Baseball. His answers to Patrick's questions were full and detailed. Daddy also entertained my questions, but I could see he was much more interested in a dialogue with Patrick, so I let them have their moments when they were together.

Little did we know how adventurous this trip was going to be. The funniest story began when I drove down to Baltimore to meet my parents from New Jersey, where I was living at the time. Patrick was spending his summer in Nashville with them. Before I arrived at the hotel, my mother called to let me know that my nine-year-old son was "running around somewhere" in the hotel. She couldn't tell me where he was, but she did say "Not to worry, we have everybody looking for him." I totally freaked out and couldn't wait to get to the hotel.

When I arrived at the hotel lobby, I was so mad and upset, I wasn't aware of how I looked to others. I saw several old black men walking around as if looking for something. One had a cane, the other was in a wheelchair, and one in particular was in a wheelchair smoking this big fat cigar. He stopped and looked at me for a moment before saying, "You must be Kimbro's daughter." I replied, "Who are you?" Instead of identifying himself, he said, "You act like him and look like him with that mean old look on your face." At that point, I smiled, because I knew what he was talking about.
He then introduced himself as Double Duty. I still didn't know who he was at that time, but when I told my dad what he had said, Daddy said, "We were roommates in Cuba while playing baseball." He went on to tell me, "Double Duty blows a lot of smoke," meaning not to pay any attention to what Double Duty said about him.

After much searching, I found Patrick in the hotel swimming pool. He had his swimming trunks on, a towel, his underwater glasses, and a backpack to transport his items. This kid had organized this trip when he was in the elevator going to the room. When he read that the hotel pool was on the second floor, he planned it out without asking my parents' permission.

My parents were supposed to keep him in Baltimore with them for a week, but somebody this cunning needed closer supervision, so I packed him up and took him back to New Jersey with me. I told my parents to enjoy the rest of the week, and I would return with Patrick on Friday. When I brought him back to the hotel, my father was quite happy to see him return. He casually mentioned that some of the other players would be glad to see him too.

I discovered the truth of Daddy's prediction that afternoon, when we prepared to board the bus that was to transport the Negro League players and their families to Camden Yards for the game. When Patrick got onto the bus, those old men applauded his return and gave him high fives as he bounced down the aisle to a seat. When I boarded the bus, they booed me, and then fussed at me, saying, "You know you ain't right taking Kimbro's grandson from him like that, Kimbro missed him."

Even Double Duty joined in their sentiments! I gave them all frowns and went to my seat; Daddy got a giggle from that. But when I look back at that moment, those players displayed genuine friendship for my father's predicament of missing Patrick that week. Although they made me the villain, it was okay, because it was wonderful to see that.

During All-Star week my father was in his glory, and reconnected with former teammates who were truly glad to see him, including Joe Black and others. Before the honors luncheon for the players started, Daddy saw Joe Black at the next table. He told Patrick to go over and tell him that he (Joe) was fat. Patrick went over and told him, and Joe Black asked Patrick, "Who is your grandfather?" When Patrick replied, and Joe saw Daddy, he laughed and told Patrick, "Go back and tell your grandfather that he owes me money." This had Joe Black and Daddy, who had heard this, both laughing.

Then Buck O'Neil came over to speak to my mother, in Spanish; Buck spoke fluent Spanish, and he and Momma conversed in Spanish until Daddy stepped in and said, rather loud, "Hey, hey, hey, speak English around here." Daddy never learned any more Spanish than he needed while he was courting my mother in Cuba, but had wanted us to learn Spanish and be bilingual. Yet I later learned it was Momma who insisted we concentrate on English. She didn't want us to be confused with both languages while we were going to school. Knowing the pain she always felt, struggling to speak English around people in general, I knew that was the subject I had to work hard on, so she would be proud of me. That was one reason it filled my heart with such joy when Buck O'Neil began to speak to my mom in Spanish. I loved Buck for that, and that memory came to me when I heard of his passing several years later. He was a class act.

As the luncheon began, you could feel that something special was going to happen. When Buck O'Neil got up to speak, you knew he was the special occurrence. It was a pleasure to hear such an articulate man speak. While he spoke, I felt transported back to another era. He was so vivid with his stories about those days they played in the Negro League, and his eyes danced when he spoke of the love of the game they all shared. He truly was the best ambassador for the game of baseball.

Later that evening, we returned to the hotel. While I

was sitting in the lobby, a small and slender elderly man came up to me and asked, "Where is your dad?" By now used to being recognized as Daddy's daughter, I told the man he was on his way down to the lobby to meet me. "That's my man," he said, "that's my man." When he saw Daddy, he embraced him with such reverence; I knew this had to be another old-time friend. I could see both had mutual respect for each other.

They talked for a long time, Daddy with the biggest smile on his face, until at one point, Daddy introduced the man as Sam Lacy, one of the most prominent journalists during the days of Negro League Baseball. Through their conversation, I heard stories that took place in Baltimore during Daddy's playing days. Later, a bit of Internet research told me that Sam Lacy was one of the most outstanding African-American and Native American journalists, with a career that spanned nine decades. He was well respected as a man who took a stand on the integration of Major League Baseball. His tireless efforts in promoting the issues of equality and fair treatment of Negro League players like Jackie Robinson and others have led many to credit him for being instrumental in the integration of Major League Baseball. Mr. Lacy wrote several articles that were read nationally. In 1948, he became the first black member of the Baseball Writers Association of America. In 1997, he received the J. G. Taylor Spink Award for outstanding baseball writing from the BBWAA, which placed him in the writers and broadcasters wing of the Baseball Hall of Fame in 1998. But on this day, Daddy and this man went on talking as if they were best friends who hadn't seen each other in years.[2]

Before the 1993 Major League All-Star Game began,

twenty-four Negro League Baseball players were paraded out to the field, wearing replicas of their team uniforms, and introduced to the fans. It was blistering hot that day, and I worried about the effects of the heat on those guys. But they seemed to all take it in stride. As each player was introduced, a giant picture of them was shown on the scoreboard while the announcer described their accomplishments as a player. When it was my father's time, he stood up straight with a huge grin and tilted his Baltimore Elite Giants hat to the crowd. The crowd, I felt, gave him the loudest response because he had played for Baltimore, and he relished this, his finest hour. Seeing this, I couldn't stop crying because no one knew that four weeks before he came to Baltimore, he had suffered another mini-stroke and his doctors had described his recovery as a miracle. My mother explained it as God's will that Daddy make this trip, a trip that brought him full circle back to the place where he spent his golden years as a player, to take his final bow. It was his time to answer the call to a much overdue call to glory from Major League Baseball, the fans, and the City of Baltimore. Within that moment, I felt the universe had adjusted itself to finally do what was so right. I have never been as proud of my father as I was that day, and of the awesome feeling that I was watching greatness when they all were honored.

During this time in my Dad's life, I discovered a strong brotherhood existed among Negro League veterans. In the scrapbook, there is a picture showing members of the Newark Eagles Baseball Club. Among those in the picture were Monte Irving and Leon Day. They simply wrote: To Kimbro from the Newark Eagles Baseball Club." Also in the scrapbook were collections of Christmas cards over a period of years from Max Manning and family, Richard Powell, and many others. Also, there was a picture of Buck O'Neil in uniform signed, "To Henry from Buck O'Neil," from when Buck was the Chairman of the Negro Leagues Baseball Museum.

Daddy went on to go to many other reunions, but as he said often, "Everything has its time." In 1997, when his health began to decline, it also seemed his time was nearing. By then, he had survived a major heart attack and several mini-strokes, but it was congestive heart failure that eventually stole his health. During his last stay in the hospital, it dawned on me that Daddy wasn't going to bounce back from this, as he had done so many times in the past. Even then, this realization wasn't real to me, because my daddy didn't ever face anything he couldn't win.

My mother and I wrestled with the fact that we should have a conversation with him about this. But one day I was in his room and the cardiologist came by to talk with him, to explain the options he had at this point to treat his condition. I will never forget that conversation, and neither will the cardiologist. The first option was to increase his medication, and Daddy said okay to this. The doctor said that option two was to change his medication to a stronger drug. Daddy said only, "I see." Next, the doctor explained that option three was to have aggressive surgery. Daddy looked displeased at that one; he was 88 years old, and I knew he didn't want that. The doctor then said, in a voice both unsure and slow, "Mr. Kimbro, if these options don't work, well ..." When he paused, Daddy jumped in and quickly said, "Well bye-bye." The doctor, at a loss for words, began to look around the room. When he looked at me, I had my face covered, not from sadness, although it was sad news, but to hide that I was giggling from the blunt response Daddy gave-classic Daddy-and the look on the cardiologist's face.

As the weeks went by, my mother asked me to make the decision on whether to put Daddy through the experimental heart surgery that the doctor suggested. Knowing my father's position on surgery, knowing he was growing more and more agitated with procedures, with tests, with doctors, I suggested no. Momma said she agreed with me, and the hospital released him to go home, to never return again.

As we left the hospital, Daddy said, "I am going to ride with you." On the drive, I wanted to talk about his options again, but he didn't. He wanted to talk about his next goal. Surprised, I said, "What is that, Daddy?" He said, "I've got to work on getting my strength back so I can drive my car again." How do you tell someone you love that they aren't returning from this path? Knowing my dad, I didn't even try. Within three days of his return home, I couldn't tell my dad anything anymore, ever. He passed early Sunday morning, while my brother Phillip was spending the weekend at the house to help out, and I was away. It was ironic that Daddy passed on the weekend I wasn't there, because I had moved back home with my parents during the summer to help my mother handle him. Once again I felt God's will, allowing that time for my brother and father to have the closure they needed.

I cried for a very long time when Daddy died. But during the funeral, I heard his voice saying, "Don't carry on too long for me cause it is already said and done, it is already said and done, my time is over." At that moment, I knew

Daddy would have been proud of me; I had told both preachers who spoke at his funeral, Dr. Revered John Cory, our family preacher, and Revered Tommy Gray, childhood friends of my brother and me, that they had only thirty minutes total to speak about my father. Daddy didn't want anyone carrying on and on; his wishes were to "say what you must and carry me on." His funeral went exactly the way he wanted it.

On March 12, 2005, another honor was given to my dad. He was inducted into the Metropolitan Nashville Public Schools System Sports Hall of Fame. I was informed of his induction by then-Director of Athletics of Nashville Public Schools, Scott Brunette, a respected friend. I don't think anyone knew at that time of the ironic significance of that induction. My father never went past a 6th-grade education, and leaving school was a devastating moment in his life. How sweet this would have been if he were alive to receive the award. I can hear his response of "well, ain't that something." He would have been very proud. Phillip and I attended the ceremony to accept the award on his behalf.

After my father passed, I had a gnawing feeling that something was left undone. I was given a vision of Daddy coming full circle and truly being at peace. One day, while looking at his scrapbook, I was inspired to put together a baseball resume for him. After looking at that resume, I concluded I needed to pursue some type of recognition for him, at least in his home state of Tennessee. There were two people who influenced me to nominate him to be inducted into the Tennessee Sports Hall of Fame: Larry Walker, the by-then former owner of the Old Negro League Sports Shop of Nashville, and James L. Smith, Jr., a Nashville police sergeant who is an amateur historian on Negro League Baseball, and the son of my best friends, James and Sandra Smith. When I mentioned the idea of doing this, both men motivated me to follow that dream and insisted I do nothing less. I knew they both had a deep admiration for my father, and both strongly felt he should be in the Major League Baseball Hall of Fame.

In submitting the nomination to the Tennessee Sports Hall of Fame, a key sports figure in Nashville told me his induction would never happen, because Daddy played in the Negro League and would face a discriminating group who had no respect for that league and its place in history.

The first nomination was denied. The next year, I solicited several letters of support, including a letter from Buck O'Neil. Although I didn't know it at the time, I later found I had the support of one of Nashville's community leaders who went on to become the first black vice-mayor of Nashville, Howard Gentry. My family was extraordinarily grateful to him and others for the successful nomination the second time. On February 11, 2003, along with other honored greats in their sports, Henry Allen Kimbro was inducted into the Tennessee Sports Hall of Fame.

The ceremony was a first-class event in which my brother and I represented our dad. Our family sponsored three tables for the event, our family table, our friends' table, and the most important table of them all, a table for the surviving Negro League players who lived in Nashville. Before the ceremony, I saw them all in the lobby with their families, and it was a blessing to have them there to share in this honor. Truly, all of them belonged in the Tennessee Sports Hall of Fame with my father.

My sister served as the family host for the table where

Mr. Butch McCord and his wife Christine, Mr. Jim Zapp and his wife Muffin, Mr. Sidney Bunch and his guest, and Mr. William "Sou" Bridgeforth and his guest were seated. When it was time for my brother and me to accept the award and induction on behalf of Daddy, I came forward to give the acceptance speech. During my speech, I turned the audience's attention to the table where they were seated and introduced each one of them. My sister later told me that something astonishing happened during that time. Although most of them were moving quite slow, and some needed help getting to their seats in the banquet hall, when each of them were introduced individually to the Sports Hall of Fame audience, they each stood up strong, and each had a spiritual aura around them. It was as if time stopped to pay homage to these forgotten heroes. My eyes teared up because I also saw my father among them, even from the podium. I was so proud these heroes were there on that wonderful night my family will always cherish.

Daddy's scrapbook allowed me to take a journey back in time and to journey back as many times as I wanted. It allowed me to become friends with many great people, especially with living legends like Jim Zapp, Butch McCord, William "Sou" Bridgeforth, and Sidney Bunch; these men inspired me. This journey has allowed me the blessing of traveling with my father through the many stages of his life. I loved who my father was, I loved who he became, and I loved telling his story from a daughter's perspective, for his story brings to life the men and women who earned a special place in history, yet were often forgotten. Above all, this journey has allowed me to honor my parents and their blessed life together. To God be the glory that I was able to make this journey with Daddy's scrapbook guiding me along the way.

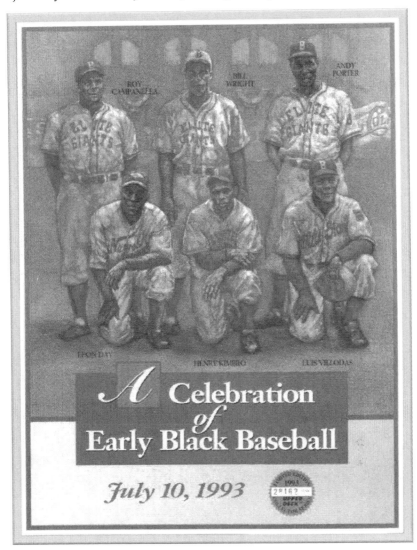

The Souvenir given at the 1993 MLB Baseball All-Star Game
Baltimore, Maryland
(Courtesy of Upper Deck)

Daddy and Sam Lacy at the 1993 MLB All-Star Game
(Courtesy of Author)

Daddy on the Right and Double Duty Radcliffe on the Left at a
Signing Session at the 1993 MLB All-Star Game Week
(Courtesy of Author)

Mr. Buck O'Neil and Mom at the 1993 MLB All-Star Game
(Courtesy of Author)

My Parents and I at the 1993 MLB Honors Luncheon for Negro League Players
(Courtesy of Author)

My Parents with Patrick and I at the 1993 MLB All-Star Event
(Courtesy of Author)

My Son Patrick and Daddy at the Hotel at the 1993 MLB Baseball All-Star Game
Baltimore, MD.
(Courtesy of Author)

My son Patrick with Baseball Great Joe Black
(Courtesy of Author)

Presented By

**National Association of Black Journalists
Sports Task Force**

to

Henry Kimbro

for Long and Meritorious Service

in Behalf of

Black Athletes

August 23, 1996
Nashville, TN

The National Black Journalists Award
(Courtesy of Author)

My Parents with Maria and Don Drew at a Negro League Players Honors Event
Atlanta, Ga.
(Courtesy of Author)

John "Buck" O'Neil
Chairman of the
Negro Leagues Baseball Museum

To   Kimba

                From Members of the Newark Eagles
Baseball Team

        Left to Right: Clint Thomas, Nancy Dickerson
Leon Heron, (Schlitz Brewing Co) Clarence Isreal,
Roy Dandridge, Rufus Lewis, Josephine Brown
daughter of "Smokey" Joe Williams, Leon Day
and Monte Irvin

My sister Maria at the Tennessee Sports Hall of Fame Induction Ceremony
(Courtesy of Author)

Daddy's Tennessee Sports Hall of Fame Award
(Courtesy of Author)

Daddy's Moment of Salute at the MLB 1993 All-Star Game Day
(Courtesy of Author)

NOTES

Introduction

1. Randy Horick. "They Might Have Been Heroes." Nashville Scene, May 2, 1996, p. 25.

Chapter 1

1. Louise Hancock interview. July 12, 2007.
2. Hancock interview. July 12, 2007.
3. Hancock interview. July 12, 2007.
4. Henry Kimbro interview. June 4, 1980.
5. H. Kimbro interview. June 4, 1980.
6. H. Kimbro interview. June 4, 1980.
7. Larry Kimbro interview. July 12, 2007.
8. H. Kimbro interview. July 4, 1980.
9. L. Kimbro interview. July 12, 2007.
10. From Baseball/Literature/Culture: Essays, 2008–2009 © 2010 Edited by Ronald E. Kates and Warren Tormey by permission of McFarland & Inc., Box 611, Jefferson NC 28640. www.mcfarlandpub.com

Chapter 2

1. Henry Kimbro interview. June 5, 1989.
2. H. Kimbro interview. June 5, 1980.
3. H. Kimbro interview. June 5, 1980.
4. H. Kimbro interview. June 5, 1980.
5. H. Kimbro interview. June 5, 1980.
6. H. Kimbro interview. June 5, 1980.
7. H. Kimbro interview. June 5, 1980.
8. http:// www.answer.com/topic/henry-kimbro. Accessed July 21, 2014.
9. James A. Riley. *The Biographical Encyclopedia of the Negro*

Baseball Leagues. (New York: Carroll & Graf Publishers, Inc.) 1994, p. 463.

10. Ibid., p. 463.

11. Brent Kelly. *Voices from the Negro League: Conversations with 52 Black Standouts.* (Jefferson: McFarland & Company, Inc., Publishers) 1998, p. 53.

12. Ibid., p. 100.

13. Ibid., p.155.

14. Ibid., p.203.

15. Brent Kelly. *The Negro Leagues Revisited: Conversations with 66 More Baseball Heroes.* (Jefferson: McFarland & Company, Inc., Publishers) 2000, p.25.

16. Ibid., p, 96.

17. Ibid., p. 115.

18. Ibid., p.139.

19. Ibid., p. 155.

20. Randy Horick. "They Might Have Been Heroes." Nashville Scene. May 2, 1996.

21. William F. McNeil. *The California Winter League: America's first Integrated Professional Baseball League.* (Jefferson: McFarland & Company, Inc., Publishers) 2002, p. 13.

22. Ibid., p. 205-206.

23. Letter from John "Buck" O'Neil, to Harriet Kimbro-Hamilton, March 8, 2002.

24. Letter from Larry Schmittou to Harriet Kimbro-Hamilton, April 16, 2002.

25. Letter from Judge Aldolpho A. Birch, Jr. to Harriet Kimbro-Hamilton, March 11, 2002.

26. Letter from Clinton "Butch" McCord to Harriet Kimbro-Hamilton. May 2, 2002.

27. Letter from Larry Walker to Harriet Kimbro-Hamilton,

April 5, 2002.

28. Letter from Ronnie Greer to Harriet Kimbro-Hamilton, September 30, 2003.

29. Brent Kelley. "The Negro Leagues: Henry Kimbro," Sports Collectors Digest, March 7, 1997.

30. Larry Kimbro interview. July 12, 2007.

31. Frazier Robinson. *Catching Dreams: My Life in the Negro Baseball Leagues.* (Syracuse: Syracuse University Press) 1999, p. 155-156.

32. Jim Zapp interview. May 30, 2010.

33. Henry Kimbro interview. June 8, 1980.

34. Bob Luke. *The Baltimore Elite Giants.* (Baltimore: John Hopkins Publication) 2009, p.04.

35. Larry Kimbro, interview. June 8, 1990.

36. L. Kimbro interview, June 8, 1990

37. Shannon Jones interview. August 3, 2008.

38. Jones interview. August 3, 2008.

39. Jones interview. August 3, 2008.

40. Jones interview. August 3, 2008.

41. Jones interview. August 3, 1980.

42. Jones interview. August 3, 1990.

43. H. Kimbro, interview. June 8, 1980.

44. Christopher Threston. *The Integration of Baseball in Philadelphia.* (Jefferson: McFarland & Company, Inc. Publishers) 2003, p. 64.

45. L. Kimbro interview. June 12, 2007.

Chapter 3

1. Luke, *The Baltimore Elite Giants*, p. 58.

2. Bruce Chadwick. *When the Game was Black and White: The Illustrated History of Negro Leagues.* (New York: Abbeville Press) 1992, p. 130.

3. Erbia Kimbro interview. July 10, 1980.

4. Jorge Figueredo. *Cuban Baseball: A Statistical History, 1878-1961.* (Jefferson: McFarland & Company, Inc. Publishers) 2003, p. 229.

5. Ibid., p. 230.

6. Ibid., _____

7. Ibid., _____

8. Ibid., p. 293.

9. Ibid., p. 295.

10. Ibid., p. 308.

11. E. Kimbro interview. July 12, 1980.

12. E. Kimbro interview. July 13, 1980.

13. E. Kimbro interview. July 14, 1980.

14. E. Kimbro interview. July 15, 1980.

15. Henry Kimbro interview. July 15, 1980.

16. E. Kimbro interview. June 20, 2003.

17. E. Kimbro interview. June 20, 2003.

18. E. Kimbro interview. June 20, 2003.

19. Mario Aguilar, Jr. interview. June 20, 2003.

Chapter 4

1. Phillip Kimbro interview. May 17, 2012.

2. P. Kimbro interview. May 17, 2012.

3. P. Kimbro interview. May 17, 2012.

Chapter 5

1. Henry Kimbro. August 6, 1998.

2. http://www.en.wikipedia.org/wiki/sam_lacey. Accessed August 3, 1993.

BIBLIOGRAPHY

Ackmann, Martha. *The Remarkable Story of Toni Stone: The first Woman to Play Professional Baseball in the Negro League.* Chicago: Laurence Hill Books, 2010.

Bready, James H. *Baseball in Baltimore*. Baltimore: The John Hopkins University Press, l998.

Chadwick, Bruce. *When the Game was Black and White: The Illustrated History of the Negro League.* New York: Abbeville Press Publishers, 1992

Dixon, Phil, and Hannigan, J. *Negro Baseball Leagues: A Photographic History*. Mattituck: Amereon House, 1992.

Figueredo, Jorge S. *Cuban Baseball: A Statistical History, 1878-1961*. Jefferson: McFarland & Company, Inc., Publishers, 2003.

Flynn, Tom. *Baseball in Baltimore*. Charleston: Arcadia Publishing, 2008.

Hamilton, Harriet. *Baseball/Literature/Culture: Essays, 2008-2009*. Ed. Ronald E. Yates & Warren Tormey. Jefferson: McFarland & Company, Inc., Publishers, 2010.

Horrick, Randy. "They Might Have Been Heroes." *Nashville Scene* 2 May 1996: 25.

Kelly, Brent. *I will Never Forget: Interview with 39 Former Negro League Players.* Jefferson: McFarland & Company, Inc., Publishers, 2003.

Kelley, Brent. "The Negro Leagues: Henry Kimbro." *Sports Collectors Digest* 7 Mar. 1997: 190-191.

—. *The Negro Leagues Revisted: Conversations with 66 More Baseball Heroes.* Jefferson: McFarland & Company, Inc., Publishers, 2000.

—. *Voices from the Negro Leagues: Conversations with 52 Black Standouts.* Jefferson: McFarland & Company, Inc., Publishers, 1998.

Lanctot, Neil. *Negro League Baseball: The Rise and Ruin of a Black Institution.* Philadelphia: University of Pennsylvania Press, 2004.

Lester, Larry; Miller, Sammy J; & Clark, Dick. *Black Baseball in Detroit.* Chicago: Arcadia Publishing, 2000.

Luke, Bob. *The Baltimore Elite Giants.* Baltimore: John Hopkins Publication, 2009.

McNeil, William F. *The California Winter League: America's first Integrated Professional Baseball League.* Jefferson: McFarland & Company, Inc., Publishers, 2002.

Riley, James A. *The Biographical Encyclopedia of the Negro Baseball Leagues.* New York: Carroll & Graf Publishers, Inc., n.d.

Robinson, Frazier. *Catching Dreams: My Life in the Negro Baseball Leagues.* Syracuse: Syracuse University Press, 1999.

Threston, Christopher. *The Integration of Baseball in Philadelphia*. Jefferson: McFarland & Company, Inc., Publishers, 2003.

Index

Index

Index

Index

Made in the USA
Charleston, SC
08 September 2015